· *Selected Poems of* ·

CLINTON F. LARSON

· *Selected Poems of* ·

CLINTON F. LARSON

Edited and with an Introduction by

David L. Evans

Brigham Young University

*I express special gratitude to the administration of
Brigham Young University and the College of Humanities for
their generous help and support for this project.*

ISBN 0-87579-167-0

Brigham Young University, Provo, Utah 84602

Distributed by Deseret Book Co., Salt Lake City, Utah 84130

POEMS

Introduction   *xi*

To a Dying Girl   *3*
Sleeping in Church   *4*
Granddaughter   *5*
Leaving Sunday School   *6*
Maiden   *7*
Mother Love   *8*
First Grader   *9*
Malfare in Late October   *10*
Everybody's Getting Old   *11*
Jesse   *12*
Homestead in Idaho   *14*
Funeral   *20*
An Old Athlete Speaks of His Son   *21*
Viewing at the Mortuary   *22*
Aunt Olive   *23*
Baby Shoes   *24*
Christopher in Church   *25*
Sisters   *26*
Scholar: Hugh Nibley   *27*
Carding: Orea Tanner   *28*
Chairman of the English Department: Richard H. Cracroft   *29*
Karen Lynn's Fan   *30*
Earl's C Street Grocery   *31*
Bed and Breakfast in Little Tew   *32*
Ely Cathedral   *33*

Belle France   *34*
Tetons   *35*
Driving into Evening   *36*
A Box of Chocolates   *37*
The Death of the President of the United States (1963)   *38*
Fred Astaire and Ginger Rogers   *39*
A Letter from Israel Whiton, 1851   *40*
The Incorrigible   *45*
Peter   *48*
The Magdalene   *50*
The City of Joseph, 1980   *51*
The Professional Christian   *54*
Jesus Vaudeville for Neo-Romans   *55*
Television Evangelist   *56*
Prime Time Personae at This Point in Time   *57*
Television Anchor Man   *58*
Hot Dog   *59*
Foreign Minister   *60*
Merit Pay Increase   *61*
Prologue to a Geriatric Honor for Forty Years of Teaching   *62*
Gallery on the Eighteenth Green   *63*
What Does One Know   *64*
General Meade of Gettysburg   *65*
Shenandoah   *67*
Reading Spenser   *68*
Coleridge   *69*
T. S. Eliot   *70*
Evening: To John Milton   *71*
Fun House Manikin   *72*
Skyscraper   *73*
Ascent from a Divider   *74*
Seven-Tenths of a Second   *75*
Machine Press   *77*
Rocket Sled   *78*
Execution of the Innocents   *79*
Football Game   *81*
Pac Man: An Enormity?   *82*

Genetic Limitation   83

Hype   84

Liquid Paper   85

Racism   86

Extraterrestrial   87

It Will Not Sell   88

Vanessa Does Her Movie "Playing for Time"   90

Terrorist   91

Nuclear Winter   93

The Closing Iris of Escape, 2531 A. D.   94

Quirky Quarks   95

The Theory of Relativity   96

Einstein   97

Virgo of the Thousand Galaxies   98

A Childish Fascination with Stars   99

The Twin Planets   100

The Dark Planet: A Prospect of the End   101

The Unified Field   104

Parable   105

Final Decision   106

Alpha and Omega at the End   107

Adonoi of the Creation   108

To the Pharaoh-Hunter K Orion   110

Ramses II of Egypt   112

The Cartouche of Ramses II   114

May: The Architect of Ramses II   115

The Handmaiden of Nefertari   117

The Pyramids of Egypt   118

Bougainvillea: A Historiography   119

I Am Om   122

Images of God   123

The First Prince   124

Hello   125

The Unseen World   127

The Morning of the First Resurrection   128

Psalm of the Last Judgment   129

Apocalypse   130

The Blacksmith's Forge   *132*
The Song of Light   *133*
Advent   *137*
The Conversions of God   *139*
    West-End Clinic, or God the Scientist
    The Gull, or God the Philosopher
    Angkor Thom, or God the Brahmin
    The Chain, or God the Catholic
    Gothic Ulm, or God the Protestant
    The Chieftain, or God the Father

Commentaries   *155*

INTRODUCTION

In an introduction like this, it seems bad form to assume that any person who picks up the volume will not already be well acquainted with who the author is and why a selection of his poems is being published. At the risk of seeming condescending to the reader who is already an initiate, I feel it important to say a little about Clinton F. Larson's importance as a writer in the American West, comment on the poems included in this volume as they relate to the rest of his works, and describe briefly the principle of organization that has guided the pattern followed in this volume.

No one should question that Clinton F. Larson is one of the most significant Mormon writers or Intermountain writers. He certainly has the most prolific poetic output of any Utahn, an output that is varied in prosody, subject, style, and purpose. Although primarily a poet and a writer of poetic drama, he also writes prose comedies and children's musical drama, short stories, traditional scriptures rendered into "modern classical idiom," and literary criticism in both prose and verse. His poems have appeared in books, periodicals, and anthologies; indeed, his "Homestead in Idaho" has been widely used in British school anthologies. Among many other places, his plays have been produced in the Pasadena Playhouse and Helsinki, Finland. Well over three million copies of his books are in use. As an LDS and Utah writer, he certainly deserves to appear in a selected edition which can acquaint even more readers with his poetic works.

His importance as a poet, however, goes far outside institutional or regional limits. His reputation as an author has nothing to do with rendering his home society in "local color." Many current writers have become tagged as "regional" because their lives and values keep them in a specific geographical locale, even though their poems are thematically and stylistically cosmopolitan and their appeal is universal: William Stafford, for instance, as an "Oregonian" or Kenneth Rexroth as a "Southern Californian." Larson's subjects are in no sense circumscribed; when he writes about man's spiritual life, it is not in terms of a prescribed theology, but with a cosmopolitan recognition of the universal range of truth. Science, for instance, he recognizes as one of the essential elements of all twentieth-century life; yet few poets show a tolerance for science, much less an inclination to use it as both subject and technique. Many of Larson's readers have been struck by his use of such materials; Nathaniel Bunker of Harvard's Widener Library, for example, has noticed that Larson refers more cogently to science in his writings than other poets with whom he is familiar. It should be recognized, however, that Larson does much more than use occasional references to scientific concepts. In bold experimentation he incorporates the very language of science directly into the fabric of his poetic lines. It may startle the unprepared reader to find a poem beginning ". . . into its compleat compaction / Singularly and vastly hot at 10^{-43} second at trillions / Of degrees centigrade, burgeoning at 10^{23}K," and even more so to discover that the speaker of the lines is God looking back at the big bang of creation through the eyes and in the language of the twentieth-century astrophysicist. But by using this technique Larson is able to bind together poetry, science, and religion in a way that can be achieved by no other means.

Of course, the use of scientific concepts and language provides only one limited aspect of his poetic variety and experimentation. Many of his poems capture with charm and simplicity the multiform reflections from the everyday facets of life. Others present with satiric wit the multitude of weird types in the modern world, from the "Television Evangelist" through the "Hot Dog" of the ski slopes to "Prime Time Personae." In other poems he confronts us with the terrors that await just beyond the fringes of our consciousness in the modern world: not just the spectacular horrors that most people discover only in headlines, like "The Terrorist" or "The Incorrigible," but the everyday possibilities on the highways ("Ascent from a Divider" or "Seven-Tenths of a Second") or in the workplace ("Machine Press"). He uses movies and film personalities, history and geography, figures of myth and of scripture—materials, that is, borrowed from all times and from all phases of human (and also inhuman) existence. And he uses the imagery of light.

If I were going to use a catchy title for this volume, instead of the baldly descriptive "Selected Poems of . . .," it would be "The Darkness Within the Light." Certainly Light, with its multitudinous meanings and suggestions, is the central image in Larson's poetry. But in most of its meanings that Light contains within itself its own contrarieties. The result is nothing like Shelley's "dome of many-coloured light" that "stains the pure radiance of eternity." Instead it is more like the scientist's laboratory spectrum. not a unuorth continuum of colors found in an abstractly pure white light, like a rainbow, but the unique spectrum of light from a specific burning source with its alternating bands of light and utter dark, identifying for the scientist the chemical composition as well as the velocity and direction of the source. Within the poems this spectrum identifies the philosophical, moral, and emotional nature of the subject.

The resulting poetry is complex in its subject matter and tonal effects. Larson is never the simple lyricist; even when he writes about children's pleasures or a colleague's cats, the resulting verse is grounded in philosophy, even theology. The values of such poetry can be great, but it does force the reader to concentrate as deeply as did the poet. Larson's poetry is strongly imbued with "negative capability," so that we seldom hear the poet speaking simply in his own person; the persona of the poem must be identified and evaluated. He shares with the French Symbolists and with other modern poets a belief that suggestion outvalues direct statement in the approach to complex truth. Because he borrows his language and images from all human activities, the reader must be aware of seeming versus true incongruities and must be willing to learn new concepts and even whole subjects. If Larson makes such demands, it is never to show off his learning or to impress the reader. His demands on himself are those of a purist who will not proceed until he has measured himself against the goal. As he has observed himself, he is an "egoist," not an "egotist." He places himself and his knowledge in the center of the work, but never to preen, never to call attention to his own sterling qualities. He is there at the center because he feels that for the poet to be uninformed, coy, or insecure is one of the worst forms of sentimentality.

In poetic technique, he is one of the few modern poets who feel that versification truly matters in poetry, so the structuring of lines, subunits, and total poems must be carefully observed; when he infrequently uses free verse, it is because patterned verse cannot achieve the goal as well. Moreover, like the better poets of almost any age, he strives for the fullest concentration in his language. As a result, his chief communication is likely to result from juxtaposed images, from subtle connotations, from the replacement of an expected word with an unexpected one, from delicate ironies, from witty verbal byplay—in short, from all types of indirection.

But if the poetry is often demanding, it is rewarding. The careful attention to detail provides a verbal texture that can give pleasure to the eye, ear, mind, and feelings together. The philosophical ground challenges, then exhilarates the mind, and the juxtapositions of light and dark draw the soul directly into the total life of man here on earth.

In trying to provide some pattern for the poems included in this selection, I have rejected such purely mechanical approaches as chronological listing or subdivision into published and unpublished poems. Although it would be obviously disruptive to set up labeled subdivisions according to theme, I have tried to provide a gradual transition from the simplest, most immediately personal types of poems, through increasingly removed and philosophical poems, into the poems that counterpoise science and religion, and finally into the poems dealing purely and distinctively with religion. But there are no sharp dividing lines; one type of subject will gradually shade into another. The very first poems I have included deal with recognizable human types that practically everyone will be able to identify with very directly: "To a Dying Girl," "Sleeping in Church," "Granddaughter." Though all of these are based on people Larson has known directly, they are presented so universally that the poet becomes removed from the sentient center and the reader takes his place almost completely. These poems are followed by a small group of others (like "Homestead in Idaho") based on people the poet read about instead of knowing personally, but where the reader identification is immediate and the implications directly on the surface. Next come poems which obviously entail people close to the poet, where the poet's presence is more obvious, poems based on his father's career as an athlete, on relatives and the poet's children or grandchildren, recognized by name ("Aunt Olive," "Sisters," "Christopher in Church"), and also on places which have played a strong role in the poet's developing sensibility ("Bed and Breakfast in Little Tew," "Tetons"). Moving away from the poet's own circle, the poems turn to historical figures (scriptural personalities like "Peter" and "The Magdalene," and eminent spokesmen for the many implicated themes of the Civil War), to national and cultural figures ("The Death of the President of the United States," "Coleridge," "T. S. Eliot") and to generalized but readily recognized current types ("The Incorrigible," "Television Evangelist"). These modern types lead us into the dark side of modern life ("Seven-Tenths of a Second," "Machine Press," "Nuclear Winter") as well as some of the lighter concerns of current technology ("Pac Man," "Liquid Paper," "Fun House Manikin"). From technology we move to science and a group of poems combining the visions of the scientist with the imperatives of religious insight ("The Twin Planets," "The Dark Planet," "Adonoi of the Creation"). Then come poems about Ramses II of Egypt and his court in a group of "Ramesside" poems which are of special significance to Larson himself. These gradually give way to poems in which the subject is entirely religious ("I Am Om," "Apocalypse," "Alpha and Omega at the End," "Advent," "The Conversions of God").

If the framework sounds mechanical, I hope that a reading of the poems will show quickly that no imposed architecture can dull the freshness, vigor, originality, and depth of the poems themselves. The one result I can hope for is that the arrangement may make it easier for the newcomer to Clinton F. Larson's poetry to get oriented briefly at the start before going on to make discoveries for himself as the poet has done in his own creative odyssey.

DAVID L. EVANS
January 1988

· *Selected Poems* ·

TO A DYING GIRL

[See commentary]

How quickly must she go?
She calls dark swans from mirrors everywhere:
From halls and porticos, from pools of air.
How quickly must she know?
They wander through the fathoms of her eye,
Waning southerly until their cry
Is gone where she must go.
How quickly does the cloudfire streak the sky,
Tremble on the peaks, then cool and die!
She moves like evening into night,
Forgetful as the swans forget their flight
Or spring the fragile snow,
So quickly she must go.

SLEEPING IN CHURCH

Lovely. Lovely. She brought her rickety bones
And her belief to church, and now she sleeps.
Hardly in the arms of Morpheus, who weeps
In envy of her peace, she nods as she atones
For every ill she thought of, amid the knowns
And unknowns of this life. A low moan seeps
From chief authority that she abridges and defeats
His charismatic rule, though he busily hones
The edge of Calvinism, grim and erstwhile,
Mulling doctrine. But Sunday is a day
Of rest, as she knows it. Who would defile
Such peace? Not I. The church is hers, a way
To house the inner light and the inner sight
Of God it proffers, not the whittling spite
Against her Christian will. Oh, lovely, lovely she,
Aging at eighty-five in the arms of her creator!

GRANDDAUGHTER

Next to tears for the supposed naughtiness
Of tipping oatmeal from her pastel bowl
And spilling milk under our haughtiness,
She displays the repentance of her soul

Over there. Her gaze is tenuous with sorrow
As she looks at the world, hoping for the best,
Arms folded to gather herself for the harrow
Of scolding. "Amen," she says in a tentative test

Of our love, grace over, but willing to pray.
I saw that the lip of her tray had tipped her bowl,
She not knowing why her oatmeal in disarray
Was so, but feeling the sackcloth of her role.

And there stand I as well with her as anywhere,
Marvelling how to keep some order at hand,
Displaying my hope glossily to keep fair
Days of charity flowing like hourglass sand.

LEAVING SUNDAY SCHOOL

Brightly pastel, as if tufting the air, she twirls
At the door, beribbons her hair, and pats her dress
Going out. As if in gossamer, she smiles distress
That her shoelaces, undone, bounce like curls
As she runs. There, by a sycamore tree, squirrels
Turn and dart before her, up the bark to impress
Sparrows, robins, and wrens observing not less
Than spring, and her especially, who furls
A lilac, with dextrous twist, around her finger.
As I say she should run, she does, down a walk,
But then I wish I had asked her to stop and talk,
To tell me why she should not solemnly linger
To consider furry and feathery creatures up there,
How she could saucily teach them how better to care
For each other.

MAIDEN
[See commentary]

So old at thirteen, she has her own room.
A change has come over her like a solemn hush
Over roses as spring becomes suddenly warm. The rush
Of color to her cheeks, signifying another loom
Of feeling that interests her, hardly invests
Our attention in petals that stray in the air
To alight at her feet, though they are certainly there.
And now, queenly, she notices our bequests
Of admiration that her eyes are skiey blue,
That she wears a trace of rouge, a natural gloss
On her lips, gems on her fingers that drew
Our attention at first, and diamonds that toss
Their glistening from the lobes of her ears.
She is more, even now, more than she appears,
Even to me.

MOTHER LOVE

The quiet book slopes
Over the tot's lap,
Where it becomes the topography
Of a meadow of flannel flowers.

Its pages,
As they turn,
Convey linear houses and trees
Embossed by a mother
Anxious for camaraderie
In the menagerie
Of her home.

She lets the children play
With pastels of gold and green
To keep their freedom,
Knowing that
Behind each image on a page,
On every lap,
On the smoothest nap,
Is the discipline
Of a hidden
Gripper
Snap.

FIRST GRADER

She can draw, or maneuver pieces of a puzzle
(Is it jigsaw, tinker, rubric?), and so confound
Adults into an amazement through which, so profound,
She cleverly saunters, neatly original, to nuzzle
Up to Merlin in a primer book, though never to muzzle
Any ilk of storyteller. Her feeling surely as sound
As thinking, she considers backyard denizens bound
By duties of affection, including birds and chuzzle-
Wits. Neatly riding whatever crest (joy, bluegrass,
Wind), she appoints discourse with dayspring blue,
Lifting forward into fairest reasoning to surpass
Our logic, offering violets to affluent us to sue
For favors for various waifs. I say, in sobriety,
That she will ever be president of a relief society.

MALFARE IN LATE OCTOBER

Well, consider it, though you may not get it.
Spooks of halloween receive it well on dole,
Itching and fidgeting with varieties of soul.
Their indigence, their witchery must let it
Come, and imps with argument for sundering
Must invest it randomly in nooks of rookeries
Of pterodactyls where they prepare their claqueries,
To be. Vine the dark and musty hours, wondering
How they are, slipping and tracking, ratcheting
In blue and orange, with scary pumpkins glowing
Wickedly with teeth, with web of all our fears
Tattering through them. Formic denizens, sowing
Wind, reap our souls, like dervishes in weirs
Of air, and upstarts, acknowledging a weird
Electorate, fulfill some destiny to beard
Medusa as she pretties up for us with treats.

EVERYBODY'S GETTING OLD

If you like what you do, arranging a career
To serve you well, you may enjoin the spilling
Years to provide your reality, which is trilling
Illusion. Your decline is steady as you fleer
Your disgust at those who slowly grind sheer
Hours like birdclocks, watching. You are willing
Always to foot and count sprockets, fulfilling
Vagaries of nothing. So, crocodile, a tear
Is yours if you cry it! Your overt will mills
Your design among the warming, wavering gutters
That you inure. But again and again sills
Of the century come. You lose. Who blesses
But you twenty when forty, forty when eighty?
All is smalling time, vanishing though weighty
As the pendulum that rotates as it swings
In your mindlight as you try to catch rings
Of the carousel, the delusion.

JESSE
[See commentary]

We stumbled up the stairs, onto the back porch,
Where Jesse's father kept his hunting gear,
His shotgun leaning against a porch screen
That puffed a mist of dust when touched or rubbed.
So Jesse said, "Look out. The step is loose."
We went in, asking his mother, Leah, for time
To ride out to the lake. With her assent,
We left, grazing the evening with whispering,
And threw blankets over the horses whose reins
We left slack to the ground. We steadied them
And jumped up easily, jostling and settling
Where best to ride. Then off into the evening,
Wresting from the near air intimacy and warmth
Of summer. And we rode down the even lane,
Grass and darkness to either side, the katydids
Sounding over the rhythm of the horses we kept
In the surer way, peering somberly as we went.
Jesse felt the defection from day and the tug
Of seeming to have lost it so early, after play.
He said: "The day was short enough; evening
Brings the sound of water up the shining sand.
Let's see, tonight, how high the dark lakewater
Must rise to touch the willows on the shore
Where the inlet keeps its secrecy." I nodded,
Softly yielding to the restraint of solemnity,
Reaching forward to the mane for firm balance.
I said, "A rift of light rests forward here.
Let's follow it." And he replied, "I find
The sallow world at the far edge of my hand,
And the restless rainwind veers across the lake.
I left my father and mother in the living room
Wondering why I leave them, even with you.
Questions glanced across their faces like shadows
Of boughs lifting in the breeze of evening.

I should return. But the leafing air grazes
My loneliness. Out there, where the evening
Fails, stars appear in the dark paling sky
Like memory returning." And we rode silently
As I heard the grasses against the hooves,
Near the lake. And I saw the lancet dark
Invade the gloss of water and the rippling light.
I looked at him askance and saw his eyes
And the gild of water draw a shining sleep
Into them. And as we returned, he softly rehearsed
The gentle inflections of light he knew. He said,
"I know the prince that stands beyond the air."
And afterwards, when in England I caught news
Of him in the random vision of words in print,
Newsprint fragile and yellowing as it seemed
To slip and fall from an envelope, I knew
He stumbled from step to porch, near the screen,
And jarred the bluesteel set of hammer and shank
That his father had left for his quick return.
And at once I felt the slow gait of the horses
Near the lake, where the lights of evening ease
And whisper into being beyond the gloss of day.

HOMESTEAD IN IDAHO

[See commentary]

I

"Solomon? Since I talked with him I've thought
Again about trying to make a go of it
In Idaho. As I say, this rainy weather
In Oregon is looking better and better to me.
The first time I met him, it was in Al's Bar,
Down the street. Five years ago, I think.
Well, you know, Al keeps a friendly place,
One where you don't mind stepping in
And acting neighborly. Well, there he was,
Down at the end of the bar. I noticed him
Because he was shaking, folding and unfolding a clipping.
'You from these parts?' I said. With all this space
In the West, it doesn't hurt to close it up
Whenever you can. He said, 'Well, no, not really,'
And kept folding and unfolding the clipping and looking
Down at his hands. When he stopped, I could hardly
See it, his hands were so square and big,
Like the farm work of his time. Besides, he took
His hat off, and you could see the white skin
Of his head, particularly near the part,
Where his hat took a settled, permanent place.
But his face had lightened to a buckskin color.
He had the look of a farmer who had seen a lot
Of land that needed working. Then it rose
From him. 'I suppose you would say from Idaho.
I wanted to homestead there,' he said. 'I tried it
Last year, or was it then? Not much money
To start with, but my wife Geneva and I and our children
Found a place. But it seemed a thousand miles
From nowhere, at least two weeks east from here.
I built a cabin from the boards I had brought
Along. Geneva said, 'Solomon, we can make it,

14

But we need money for spring. Go back to Tamarack
And leave us here.' Then I told her how I felt.
But she said, 'We can make it with the provisions we brought.
Go back, Solomon. By spring, we'll have a start,
Then a barn by those trees, cows grazing there,
And a house like we've wanted, beside a stream.'
Well, the way she looked, her eyes imploring,
And her soft brown hair, and her hope, how could I
Say no? So off I went, Geneva waving to me
Until I was out of sight. It was the hardest thing
I have ever done to look around and see
Where I was going. I worked at Tamarack
Autumn and winter, numb from wondering
How they were, all alone out there, and wanting
To get back to them. April finally came,
And I loaded the wagon with everything we needed,
Dresses and dry goods, shoes and ribbons besides.
I travelled as hard as I could, considering the horses,
And kept looking and looking for the smoke far off
In front of me, coming from the chimney,
To tell me I was near. But I never saw it.'
He looked again at the clipping in his hands,
Smudged and yellow, and said, 'When I got there,
It looked like autumn and winter had never left,
The snow still hanging on the roof, the door
Open, nothing planted, nothing done,
And then I went inside, to see the dusty cribs
And Geneva, still against them . . . and the floor
Red and dusted with shadows. And I was here,
Trying for money so we could get started. . . .
I couldn't stay out there.' And he looked at me
As if pleading for help, then down into his hands,
Unfolding and folding the clipping as if by doing it
He could wear out his sorrow."

II

The colors of the sun against the hills
In the evensong of life, and yet another
Year had gone. The colors crept down
Like frost and the glory of God, intermingling
In them night and day. All was over
When the family saw them, over like the evening
Wind. In the meadows and clusters of pines
It whispered to the edge of the sullen earth,
In the seethe of knowing, under the shaken plume
Of knowledge. Solomon and Geneva saw
The land cut, as it were, for them, a place
For them between the great divide and the sea.
There, he said in the voice of conscience, there
Is our home, or the hope of it. Geneva,
Can it be that home if we settle here?
A half of a year will make it ours if we stay,
She replied in the moment of seeing him
As she wished him to be. And then in resolve,
Let me stay the winter with the children
While you work in Tamarack, and so
It was out, the only way of keeping
The land. Where in the flicker of grey is death,
The wandering light, release? I want this home,
She said, in the tolerance of a breath, and I
Shall stay. Where is the imperious will but fast
Against the land that holds them? To Tamarack,
He said, bright as possession, like the coin of having
Mastery. There is my knoll where home
Shall be, not this cabin of our duration
As we should not be, itinerants in hope of more.
A winter more, she said, and it is ours,
The gaze of meadows, the water and soil
Urgent for grain, the quiet sky, and the light
Lazy as spring. Our home! And I shall keep it,
Winter through, she said, as if it were no winter,

But a day of rest. And then beside him, their children,
Or in his arms, awake to happiness. The future
Declined from that day and would not rest,
But as a bole of pain grew into that tower
Of resolve and broke it easily, sacred
As a sacrifice. He said, then think of me
In Tamarack, and turned to what he needed
Away from home. Geneva? The subtle portrait
On a stand beside a bed. The wisps
Of hair she flicked to clear her face, brown
As the veil of earth, eyes quizzical as worry,
But light as a soft morning, her body lithe
And restless, supple to the rule of God.
And Solomon? A name like a fetish he tried
To honor, but not as a patriarch, more
Like a seer: angular as a fence or cross,
Bending as he seemed to fit, concern
Like an agony to please, a burden
To his clothes that could not shape themselves,
And altogether like the square largeness
Of his hands. Together, they kept the cabin
Like a tidy loom where they would weave
The colors through their bright fidelity.
Their children? Hard to presuppose or know,
But theirs. Such small alliances, wont
To shimmer with translucent light, a guess
Of women that might have been, of course like her,
She whispered what he might take, advice
Hanging from her words like surety.
And he, the slight concerns of food and health
Like the hundreds of miles that would intervene,
And for safety the gun and knife in a drawer,
Nearby. Then the wood for winter near the door,
Neatly stacked, and provisions in the loft
And ready. What else? What else but land
Beyond their vision, the canyons, and peaks like clouds
In the thin blue haze, and time. He turned, ready,

Holding her with one arm, as he pulled
His horse from grazing to the suggestion of the miles
Ahead, and leaned to kiss his children, and then
Away, easily in the saddle, gazing back at her,
The children, cabin, everything diminishing
As he moved, and he waved, and they, in the slow
Desperation of goodbye. He could not turn forward
For seeing them there, until they were taken from view
By a vale beyond their meadow sinking into darkness,
And they were gone. From that time on he pieced
The events of time together like fragments he could not
Understand, though the evidence impaled the past
Like needles dropping suddenly through his inquiry.
There must have been a disturbance beyond the door.
And she left the cabin with the gun on her arm.
The sharp wind of October against her frailty
Where she shivered in the grey dusk. The rising
Wind, then the thunder over the plain that shook her.
She went into the darkness of a shed, wildly
Gazing. Then the severe and immediate rattle
Behind her, and the strike behind her knee, the prongs
Of venom there that made her scream. Now
The whirling thoughts for Solomon or help
From anywhere. Bleed the poison out.
Go slowly, she told herself, and bleed the poison
Out. Stumbling to the cabin, she opened the door
In the glaze of fright and found the drawer that held
The knife. She sat, livid against the lightning,
To find the place to cut. Nowhere to see,
Behind and under, but she felt the red periods there.
A piece of kindling for a brace, a cloth
For tourniquet. She took the knife and swept it
With her hand. But the chickens in the shed.
They must not starve. A few steps back
To the shed, and she emptied a pail of grain
And opened the door. As she moved, she held
The stick of the tourniquet numbly against her leg.

Slowly, slowly to the cabin, then wildly in
To seize the knife. She held it against her leg
And with a gasp twisted it in. But too deep!
The blood pulsed against her hand, again,
Again, no matter how tightly she twisted the stick
To keep it in. It spread on the rough floor
As she felt herself weaken, the waves of blackness
Before her eyes. The children! What will happen
To them? she cried to herself. The lamp flickered
At the sill. What good is the need and planning now?
Tears for dust. The girls will starve to death
In the clatter of the wind, and the light of afternoon
Will carve through their sallow loneliness.
They will lie here and cry for food, and no one will hear.
The waning fire, the gusts at the filming window.
Solomon! Forgive me! What can I do?
What else can I do? She took the gun again
And turned it to the crib, propping its weight.
She looked at them as they slept, arms lightly
Across each other. You will be with me,
She whispered to them. The trigger once, then again,
The flat sounds walling her against the error
That they would live beyond her careful dying.
The gun fell from her. She crawled to the bed
In the corner and, taking her finger, traced
In blood on the white sheet, "Rattlesnake bit,
Babies would star—" and the land fell away
Beyond her sight, and all that she was collapsed
In an artifice of death that he afterwards saw.
Solomon!

FUNERAL

What is this sudden hiatus,
Lapse, or interregnum
In which you depart like a flown
Swallow? I turned,
And you were not there,
And you kept going
My memory of memory
Going, vanishing, until you were past
Like the fervor of years
That turns the systems
Of philosophic fright
Into the deltas of God.

AN OLD ATHLETE SPEAKS OF HIS SON
[See commentary]

The leap is over; fame recedes,
The echo of forgotten deeds:
Cups, once eloquent, are dumb,
Idly staring, halt and numb;
The glowing laurels of the race
Wither in their cryptic space.

Lost honor finds pretense a gain,
Displays a mask, but hides the pain.
The lad who reveled in defeat
Sprang beyond the old deceit
And caught the image of his heart
Rinsed golden in his striving art.

The rigid resolution's mine,
Like iron cast along the spine;
Though it can never break or bend,
It shatters me before I mend,
And I, dissembled, wear a husk,
A vanquished icon in the dusk.

His pace exults, his gathering run
Assails the ramparts of the sun
That sunder prisms as they meet
The bursting spikes that lift his feet:
The mark! He leaps where cirri drift,
Blazing, golden, wind-swept, swift!

VIEWING AT THE MORTUARY

Implausibly fine, the locks of her hair
Shimmer like grain in the summery fields,
Like years that embrown the virgin land
Fallow and even for days that are fair.

For sleep that is fair she quietly longs,
Breathless to live in the realms of night,
Skipping and poising for the longer play
Beyond the day and the threshold of songs.

Her voice is low as the whispering wren's,
As quiet as listening worlds of the sky,
The shadowy fields, the fountains of light.

Lashes closed, she leaves the paths and the years
That brought her here for effusions of hymns
That still the wind-tousled locks of her hair.

AUNT OLIVE

So much like her mother, she winks a carousel
Of wit into being, and in rounds of her intent
We listen to a harmonium of stories godsent
In lyrical belief. How fine it is, in the spell
Of what she affirms, for us to see how well
She involves our inclinations! As we repent
Of a graying canvassing of mind, we vent
A sullenness that somehow learned to dwell
In us for spite. Look there! A starry midway
Illumines nearby stalls where we may spend,
And yet keep, wit of whitegold, dividend.
As we further learn of her, we see the play
She performs in settings of her fair,
Spilling timbrel sapphires through the air.

BABY SHOES

The baby shoes about which I always maunder
Were in a box at Mother's (a cardboard cache,
As it were, of tender memories) with a sash
That I must have proudly worn to wander
Across a stage—there assigned to ponder,
To look like a veritable saint, ready to thrash
A patriot's enemies (if I could), to trash
The spirit of its waywardness, and to launder
Sin before antecedents of Bills particular.
Well, these shoes wherein I tottered were kept
As reliquaries by her, as she, funicular
For my ingenuous transport, saddened and wept
At any reluctance in me to get ahead or rise
In Christian soul's profession. So prize,
Like me, beginning in shoes, and in standing
For

                    —Clinton F. Larson

CHRISTOPHER IN CHURCH

My mommy's speaking in this church.
   She's left me with a relative,
   My father. So I use an expletive
To get attention and begin to search

For my train. It's in Mommy's purse.
   Down the aisle I go, "Choo! Choo!"
   And up stairs on my knees to view
So many folks facing me. I rehearse,

"Choo! Choo!" grab her dress and legs,
   And look at them below the small talk
   Drone. "Bzz!" I drag my chalk
Across the carpet as she begs

Me not to, kneeling down. Escaping,
   I become a tall giraffe swaying
   On seats or a gray coyote baying
To the choir, and then, draping

Myself over a bench, I hoot and rail
   As she holds me near, blushing.
   But I break loose, pell mell rushing
To the pipe organ, where I sail

Into the scrim, tumble over feet,
   Tromp the keys, drifting sand,
   And, delving for a rubber band,
Flip it at a deacon. I repeat

My repertoire as the choir of hoods
   Scatters. I wish I had my Tommy
   Gun, with pellets. Come on, Mommy.
Let's lock horns and trumpet in the woods.

SISTERS

So much unalike and yet the same,
Each buoyantly respects the other's name:
Susan, Diane—Di and Sue,
Who each for each other must ever renew
The finest refined dissimilation,
As if dye were their emulation
In which blue iridescence
Were kept as nominal presence
Diverging from other especially to each
And into each other until the reach
Of affection must ever ensue,
Ever in diaphanous light.

SCHOLAR: HUGH NIBLEY

A Latin Quarter of erudition, you teem
Antennae and lecture all those like whom
You aren't—hoping for better, lacking room
Even for the time, freighting what may seem
Mere errata, or burrs with which you ream
The bore of students who erringly assume
That you are but a factual cassock—doom
To evanescent grades of which they dream.
But cozener Italianate, of scholarly aplomb
A Saint, witching facts with divining rods,
You lecture serially to stuff such pods
As open quickly to the light they gather from
The conscience of your inquiry, for you spin
Your silk through disarray as discipline.

CARDING: OREA TANNER
[See commentary]

She faces squarely up to idea, class, and student,
Finds kidswool everywhere, and begins to sort
Deserving lots into bins where sharp and prudent
Study discerns the likelihood of excellent report.
She intimately cards for quality. Willy-nilly,
Like raw wool, beggars her, and it will languish
Under her scrutiny as fairly innocent or silly
Until, becoming corrigible in students' anguish,
It smooths into the spindling that she observes.
Never was there such a one to arrange so much
What students should be, poaching on wary reserves
Of competence that she detects, their nonesuch
Gathering wool abandoned as from unfair game,
So they spin her aery cashmere fair for fame.

CHAIRMAN OF THE ENGLISH DEPARTMENT: RICHARD H. CRACROFT
[See commentary]

You are a compromise, but bedrock as Americana,
So studiously humble that two fluencies vie
In you, sonority and litotes. Though the elfin
With a Western flair prevails, you are comely shy,
And we bless your bones on your eminence for not
Escheating the style of either, whatever course
You run. Ah, mild felon, we know something of you,
Despite intrigue of plot and theme in your theatre
Aboard the River Queen! What olios for doubly
Marking twain on us! How paradoxical that you
Should wear your chaps and spurs, declaiming sotto
Voce on the boards in hues of gold and peppermint
That we, improvident, should hear a distant angelus
And see the shorelights of reality! You gave us
Fairest warning from the dock and stern, where
You applied congeniality to stint our laissez faire
And get us to embark, though we knew your charm
And boardwalk business hustled us. Furthermore,
We have in mind the lore that will last and last,
Enshrined as it is by supervening scholarship:
You bolster and confirm, in every happy hour,
Your cast of homespun idlewilds.

KAREN LYNN'S FAN

Against invisibility, it slows, delivering
   Impress of lightness whenever it moves,
   And whenever it moves it pulls and grooves
The air. See, in a mist, shivering,

It draws, compressing! Ends of spines
   Leaving impressions of barest vacuum
   Abroad in a shimmer, thin in the room!
Billowing, drawing, it gathers, defines

Its spreading hues, pastel on gauze,
   Opening still and nearly invisible,
   And I have seen abroad an indivisible
Will carefully open in a shift or pause

Of icy conversation to gather, slow,
   And draw opinions in, subsuming them
   Easily as one might hear a verbal stem
While words, unspoken, reign as though

Who opens them compresses an unseen
   Atmosphere after spinning sheerest gauze
   That hovers there. What frail cause
Will draw the hand and make us lean

To favor it, involving us as it moves?
   Or, dissembling incipience, she hovers and hums
   So patiently that when our sapience comes
It comes repining.

EARL'S C ST. GROCERY

You enter and find him between the carrots and Quinsana,
Blinking and decorative. Aware of each item,
He lives for his patrons in the panorama
Of his largesse, shelves full of the totem
Packages, cans, bottles, the heady displays
Carefully aligned where, possibly, he prays.

He looks up at you, inquisitive as a list
For your sustenance, but what can you offer?
The cryptic weather. And in the mist
Of his behavior he agrees, like a coffer
Against the hours of his lonely plight
From morning into the vast, confining night.

He rules here, Earl, for the occasion
That someone happens by with a dime
To find some little thing, provision
Or string or spool, or moments of his time,
Under the lonely swan's neck light
Glowing here, but leprously white.

We learn he dies, pallid from the work.
Failing, not remembering, he is taken
Away, stumbling in the mill of those who shirk
Accounts receivable that must lie forsaken.
So he falls, brittle and shattering
Among condolences, like feet that are pattering.

BED AND BREAKFAST IN LITTLE TEW

Fence and stonework remind one to be hesitant
About inquiring as to rates. Inside, blossoms
Lend solemnity to a gray arcade that patterns
Vines, that lift a lyric light into being
From tapestries of morning's dust from a road
That curves into a foyer of a rose garden
Near an amphitheatre of trees. An arch is there
To see but not to approach, and one guesses
From a portal in this domain who might
Have gone there to consider the covenants
Of a village where cottages nestle amid centuries.
One turns to see the wife of the proprietor
Kneading bread on trays for baking in an oven
Nearby and ready. She smiles as I knock
At the threshold of the open door and approaches,
Smiling, to greet me in the entry hall.
Do you have room? I ask, and a blossom,
As if of ancient gentility, nods in a vase
From a wave of air that came from treetops
And fled into the crevices of pastel light
To render my attention momently away. Yes,
She says, and I follow her as if a cavalier
Who has stopped on his way to Woburn Abbey,
Where Russell awaits the resolution of the King
To assign the Grand Duke to the field of Waterloo.

ELY CATHEDRAL

[See commentary]

Moors around, this worship of architecture
    Is the Calvary of a cross of Christ
    That rose from a gospel that enticed
Flocks of souls to let it rise, imprimatur

For skies; the storied cross, in elevations
    Of a resurrection, is taller than a mound
    Of arches, and the lanterns round
Must balance and bear sturdy intimations

That God is very near; the lantern must keep
    The skiey tree on beams of oak
    Erected from the faith of folk
Who sun in glory like the sower who reaps

A harvest after seasons of richest summer.

BELLE FRANCE

From Marseilles to Calais in the domain
Of diamond spring, belle France has lain
Like vineyards, in the incipience of rain,
Misty warm unto the Pyrenees and Spain.

What is it but wonder of fair Aquitaine
In the very air? Hedgerows now abloom,
A window open, singing from an inner room,
Porcelaine and lilacs, and radiant perfume.

The maze I wander in, like misting rain,
Is pastel and palest blue, as in Cezanne.
The subtle rift of morning is sun and span
Of light where the violet and jasmine fan

Of white Versailles encumbers rain
And opens, hue on hue. Who has known
Belle France in her curvatures of stone
That grace the leewardings of monotone

Under spindrift noon? Songs of the air
And fair romance have come, in illusion
Everywhere until, in their suffusion,
I keep them, in their bright profusion,

As my inner fare, O fair and melody,
As if the horn of Roland sings afar
For the emperor Charlemagne.

TETONS

Stacked largely clear before the eyes,
Sierra too brazen for common belief,
They were and are stone windreef,
Cirque and light, the shadowed size

Of passing cloud, O will of noon
To charge the air close by to revise
Flow of vision as we devise
The mind to remember the rune

Of being. Vale and wind, pines
Against gray, water an inkling
Of blue, and there a ravine tinkling
Rain in trees as dark defines

The sound of evening where moraine
Mounds from lake and fields of larkspur,
Willows wavering, marsh and lure
Of inlet, shore, and the hovering rain.

DRIVING INTO EVENING

The dusk, and, afar, clusters of towns emit
Wavering lights like companion galaxies, and softness
Past dusk, softness of air eases them into languor.
And where shall I go as the dim glow of the road
Darkens, headlights reaching forward into and over
The dark? Alone, and the hazy feeling of being
Alone at dusk, the dim fields beyond aglimmer,
Grass beyond swept and paling with shadowy silver,
Each house of windows the pale of gold. Lost
Sounds are afield, and evening is prayer in the ceiling
That overbends the silence, my pilgrimage
Wending as I move into sacristy, where sanctity
Is the breathless air. Were I to reach afar,
I might touch the townships of Nevada, Mesquite
And Logandale, as they cool from the transient fires
Of sun, green fields beside the desert gold
And the intimacy of cactus palms. Wavering,
The leaves glisten as bundles of silver. And were
I to reach farther still, to Vegas of the crown
Of light, America in the reign of Hyperion,
Victorville away, and the crest of El Cajon
Far, in the ripple of mountains, vision would be
Night as a diamond, night as a sapphire,
Starring like Orion to keep the orient of light.

A BOX OF CHOCOLATES

[See commentary]

The rum of these chocolates scents their array.
The boxy caramel lies in a dusky brown cup;
The cherry, with smooth of satin, rounds up
To bequeath itself with a garden's bouquet.
So I gather it slowly. I, who quaffed whey,
Sometime entered a Taj Mahal to dally and sup,
And now, topping off servings, fairly chirrup
To see what I see like a cheerily busybody jay.
The liqueur of cherry flows as I nip a quadrant
And makes me pop it in whole. This momentum
Acquires Moment, Occasion. Has ever a fondant
Impressed such a nonesuch who, now so quantum
For handsfull, becomes less selective, assuming
The season to be jolly and resuming so quickly
His ecstasy to bloat his cheeks for all winter.

THE DEATH OF THE PRESIDENT
OF THE UNITED STATES (1963)

The sunlight gleamed among the thronging streets
    Where he turned and passed to find a sudden way,
The pitching storm of sorrow, the floating sheets
    That silenced him and wrapt him from his day.

We start, and hear in the hum of coursing time
    What time will not disclose, except bristling
And secret in a rifle's clipping mime
    Of death, the spurt and shot, the bullet whistling.

Darkness, and all is gone, against the seat,
    Cradled there. The wild shock, waving
Away, stills us as if yesterday were neat
    And prim a thousand years ago, craving

To be born again and live again a better way.
    We cannot hold it in one waning hour,
And it is gone, slipping from us where he lay
    Dying, in the envy of time, the silent tower.

FRED ASTAIRE AND GINGER ROGERS

[See commentary]

With the proficiency of a bending willow, he takes
Her by the waist and dips her, overbending,
And glides like savoir faire for all our sakes
Into episodes of easy motion and extending
Grace with such obvious panache he breaks
The commonplace into sticks and bits, sending
Dreams as barter for better ones, strewing flakes
Of color to glitter like pastel leaves wending
Earthward to be among us. Whatever makes
Existence is so improved, whatever impending
Glamour nearer us. His glance forsakes
All else but her as he lifts her over lakes
Of halftone blue below heavenly-attending
Indigo. Pale starlight of the sun's pretending
Seems a dimming glow as he enfolds and takes
Her lightly away for keeping and suspending
In magenta, shimmering. His tie is white,
His tuxedo flowing black, his ease of night
The evidence and preeminence of their lending
To the shadowing of light the spindrift shadows
Of a solitaire.

A LETTER FROM ISRAEL WHITON, 1851

A crest of wind runs and rustles through the piñons
Below the butte, and it is evening; the moss-green shade
Glimmers with lancets and gems of the afternoon sun;
The fields beyond glow yellow-gold; and the overcast
Of blue dims pale and like powder in the air
Fails away into the recesses of light and time.
I sit before a candle that tips its flame
From the door, and I write . . .

> *Dear Mother:*
> *I received a letter from you the 8 of May.*
> *I was very glad to hear from you but I had to wet*
> *The letter with tears. You are a good Mother to me.*
> *Their was a letter came from Father too.*

I crease them at the edge of the desk, splinters
Shifting the pages awry . . .

> *I and Eliza have not forgot what you told us*
> *Before we started our journey, If we was faithful*
> *In the Gospel of the Priesthood, we should be instrumental*
> *In the hands of God, of turning the hearts of the Children*
> *To the Fathers. My health has been good every day*
> *Since I left home; I am tough and herty, enjoying*
> *Good health and this I am thankful for as usal.*

There in New Haven, the bank of pillows and the skin
Like the river sand beyond the sheeting water
That subtly rises and fails, drawing grains
In the tumult of recession, and the eyes sudden
To see me near, from sleep, and my going away
Beyond the doors that she sees closing.

> *Eliza kept all my clothes in good order,*
> *She was a good woman to take care of things.*
> *I do not know what I should have done to travel*
> *Without her, we had a team of our own, one yoke*
> *Of oxen and 2 yoke of cows.*

Over the plains from Laramie, west, the bow of mountains
Far to the south, and I write as if there, receding
Into the blue and golden undulations of distance,
Away from home and farther still to the great Divide
Of the land, and, down the reaches of the far slope,
The canyons appearing between the walls and towers
Of rock and the high vales of the wind and the wisps
Of cirri against the high flanges of stone . . .

> *We took in Sister Snow and her little boy*
> *To carry through to the valley for 75 dollars,*
> *When we got about 300 miles she died*
> *With the Cholery. Her husband was to the gold*
> *Minds and was a coming to meet her to the vally*
> *In the fall, but I heard from him; he has been sick*
> *In the Sutters' gold minds and has not come yet.*
> *By having Sister Snows things in my wagon*
> *I had to by another yoke of oxen when I got*
> *To Fort Carny where I got my cattle, because*
> *She was foot sore and could not go, for 55 dollars.*

The oxen before me, I watch the rhythm of the wagons
Tipping and heaving, and the finite dust
Settles in our wake, paling the sage on either
Side, and after. I am the measure of that journey,
Never to return, and here where the soundless sky
Drifts from the still clouds, and where it goes
I see the quiet periods of stars and the sleek
Heaven of that other certainty . . .

> *It was very bad for Eliza to have sickness*
> *And death in her wagon on such a journey.*
> *We see thousands and thousands of bufalows*
> *Moving in great heards; we kill some and had*
> *All the meat we wanted and it was as good*
> *As dried beef. We kill some antaloope, an animal*
> *As big as sheep; they was as good as mutton.*
> *Manly Barrows kill a good many rabits because*

He had a shot gun; I shot some sage hens
With Manly's gun. We see some raddle snake;
A young man got bite by one, but got well,
Very early one morning there was one run under
Our wagon and they kill it. We see Indians
In droves without number; one rode up to my wagon
And give my Eliza some blake Cherrys
And she gave him two crackers. They all ride
Horses and have long slim poles fastened
To there horses to carry there game.

From the plain I see the declivity to the stream
As we brake the wagon with poles, to the water's edge,
Then easily into the cold, the oxen threshing for footing
On the stony bed; I steady the wagon, reaching
From my horse to the buckboard, but over it goes
Like a vane against the current and the rills
Of cold, and Eliza sinks there before I catch her,
Her skirts the mantles of darkness, laden with water.

And she gazes wildly at me when I right her
And help her to the bank. She shivers as I right
The wagon from my saddle, and in the evening
I touch the question in her, of the exposure and cold
Of September, and the wind. She shivers again, trying
Against the cold . . .

We got to the Vally about the middle of October.
I work one yoke of my cattle, the old brindle some.
A cold storm come and one died. We have
Some brown sugar that we brought from St. Louis.
Wheat is worth 3 dollars a bushel, beef 10 dollars
A hundred and maybe potatoes 1 dollar a bushel.
There is grist mills and saw mills in the Valley a plenty.
The wheat on the ground bids fair for a good crop;
They raise from 40 to 60 bushels to acre;
After harvest they plow in the old stuble
And next summer get a great crop of wheat

Without sowing and this they can follow up
Year after year.

Eliza, you lie there, under the window, the last sunlight
Over your hands, and I cannot see where you
Must see, the piñons flickering like lashes
Over your eyes, the fire of embers waiting in the ash
White powdering over them . . . You lie there,
Tucked in the quilt you made for us in New Haven,
Still as the evening before the crest of wind . . .

My Hunter finds teem and seeds and tools and land
And I have one half of the crop and give him
The other half in the shock. I have 18 acres of wheat
On the ground, Mother, it looks fine up to my knees.
We have good meetings every Sunday. Eliza is . . .
The Vally is 100 miles long and about 20 wide
With the river running through the middle, called
The River Jordan and Mountains all around
The Vally higher than the clouds.

But Eliza is still as I write, and I must only
Listen. I, Israel Whiton of the Salt Lake Valley,
Write this letter to you, Mother, from the canyons
And the butte above my land; it is a leaf
From the spring before we came, as both you and Eliza
Know, unanswerable except in the signs that come,
That I cannot seek. So I give it to the wind
From the tips of piñons or the butte, and it lifts
Away, and I try to see it as it diminishes
Away, then vanishing though I know it is there,
As you know better than I, Mother. . . . And it will rise
Beyond the golden seal and touch the white hand
In the cirri pluming the Oquirrh crest west
Over the sunset, and it is as if I take a veil
Full in my hand as I write, as if to let it yield
To the days consecrated to the journey west
That holds me aloof from all I have ever known,
The East and the cities of my common being,

As I am here, in Zion, wondering about you
Who cannot respond except in the barest hints
Of being that lift over me and show me the way
To yield and rise into the Kingdom, the sky
And the land like the white silver spirit
That we know but is fathomless before us
And indefinite as the planes of God rising
Into the sun. . . .

With love,
Your son Israel

THE INCORRIGIBLE

Draper, Ralph, inmate of Block 4,
Adjudged incorrigible, when eighteen
Was given to know not to cache blasting caps
In the shed behind the Draper house;
That set of mind which turns to diametricity
Swung, and the caps were kept, sheathed
In brass, secreted, of course,
In the shed, an item of sin
And defiance.
Little Glen, brother, diseased, who, because of a fever
Could pull out
His hair in bunches, to the awe of his friends,
Spied the box of caps, pulled it down,
And dallied with its contents:
We saw him by a tree,
Sheathed in blood,
His fingers at his feet,
And stubs of fingers spraying blood,
Held rigid, like a sleepwalker's,
And he, baying with pain,
Blasted and blinded, quarried, blown,
The smell of powder infusing his hair,
Rocked with disbelief,
Waving a thumb dangling by a shred of skin.
The keening, useless women got him in,
And in the bedroom, he, writhing, left a memento,
A swath of blood, a crescent, on the wall,
Indelible beneath the sheaths of wallpaper
Added since.
Ralph, whose convolutions probe an everlasting squint,
Balds in his cell,
Awaiting resurrection morn, the prison break,
Salvation by a saw, the jimmy, the gat,
And other necessary devices designed
To subdue or maim recalcitrant guards.

The savior is a fence, an arranger,
A faultless planner;
It is he who has connections,
Parlays influence, and wears a pin stripe suit
Draped smoothly from his adequate shoulders;
It is he from whom the promises flow, and, in fine,
The everlasting "Yeah!"
The word, the resolute reality,
Recourseless finality,
Beneficent he,
Object of adulation, supplication,
Shriver, the squinting dispenser
Of the good thing and the easy buck,
Embodied rationale, the aberrant messiah,
He, the exponent of the flawless prison break
In paradise, for Draper, Ralph, No. 64320,
Gnawing bars in Cell Block 4,
Despite the caries in his basic bone,
Unfilled, uncauterized in some infinitude of hell:
I.e.,
We stood in the pool, knee deep, as a boy
Was dragged to the sand, unbreathing,
The valves of lungs unresponding to the water
Blocking the labyrinths of veins and tubes.
No. 64320 announced his candidacy
As resuscitator, resurrector
On the sand,
The sand caking on the film of water
Over the skin and in the hair.
Crimen omnia ex se nata vitiat:
His hands strike and press the ribs
Resistless:
They hush quicker than the breath,
Remote hypothesis of water;
Staccato, uneven,
They batter the filming sac for air,
Depressed.

Mouth in sand, the face blears with death:
Distinguenda sunt tempora.
"No, no . . . slower, slower!
Let him breathe!
Rhythmic! rhythmic! "
We saw him die, the mother tangling
The pulmotor the police had brought,
A ceremony to the scene in sand.
She kneeled and wept,
And No. 64320, gauche ape,
His airless eyes gnawing ignorance,
Hulked on the fringe, covered himself,
And skulked home, the vestige of a man.
Hysteropotmoi,
Chimney-wise:
Identitas vera colligitur ex multitudine signorum.

PETER

I know you are he who in the vale
Spoke of the dove and the water,
But why rankle the Sanhedrin and Rome
And me that I should follow you?

You speak in the vale, in the air
That stirs over the graves
Of our captivity.
The convention is old to us,

But in the dust we sift the ages
Nameless to Elohim
That eddy now in the sun
And settle at your feet.

Find me in the image
Of the full sail and mast
I have forsaken, forsaken as home,
For I wander as your voice

Gathers me from the net you cast
That I take and cast for you.
My soul awaits the storm
Of your prayer in me:

At least the discontent, the wish
That bathes in the blood of light!
Now trees close round the sky,
And in this long vale

Of graves, the luminous sound
Of leaves over stone;
Your sign is the spar of my bone
Though you hold me alone

In the chastening glimpse of your hour
That I never may wander:
Master, though strong, I am weak,
A vane in the wind.

THE MAGDALENE

I am here, waiting for you,
Asking for you to come,
But not as you are in your fame,
But as the hurry of leaves, forgotten.

There! The tumult of going
Lilts on the threshold of sound
As if your voice hints of the coming
Foliage of thorns.

The night bristles the whispering
Vengeance of giving, the power
Rising like the delicate hand
For the nail. The list of the head

For God, you listen to hymns
Crackling for flame, but calm
As the woodsman sleeping
You fallow the coming pain.

I am here, waiting for you,
When the obsession is over
And left in the leafless tree:
Where are the turning and fleeing

That are ever the finished God?
I am here, waiting for you,
Under the tree, waiting for the touch
Of its leaves.

THE CITY OF JOSEPH, 1980

What is this soft array of leaves and light
But morning? The sky opens with the wind
That caps the upper branches like spume,
Whiteness over them sweeping mist that rises
From meadows. And now what is the array of light
As one looks down upon the city's scape
Of buildings? The places where Joseph came
To find his Zion are in the spell of prophecy,
The sound of vision, and moments of his certainty.
One could believe that trees and buildings might be
Alike if through half-closed eyes the gathering
Of overcast and light might yield green and ochre
Steadily as earth's visions appear around them
And surely as the events of time that brought
The few together in a home to harvest
Centuries of tendency. What tendencies hover
In a prophecy or dream? The path in a glade
May be the boulevard, and a holy place
May be the place of sacrament, where visions
Come and elide distinctions that diminish
The prospect of meaning. The holy place may be
A room, a shelter of trees, a lake where white
Flickers through a scape of gray and green,
As if moraine where suddenly the crest of land
Keeps the air calm or fleeting. Joseph,
The few began the order of the Son of God,
Elijah and Melchizedek of Salem near at hand,
The plates of gold before them in whose radiance
The time became a sepulchre, language
The spirit before them, fluid in its power,
The dust of gold from ages of Teotihuacan
And the sunburst on a floor receiving sun
And prophecy from the angels of the gold
And turquoise. Canyons open, glistening
Red and green, cliffs and mesas in a curve away,

The distant mists of glory azure–lidded
And hidden in the vision of an ancient city,
Zarahemla, where towers held the words
That Nephi rendered on India gold. O city,
Your subtle glades of light, your boulevards
Open outward always as if to receive
The steady radiance of sun and sunburst,
Of Arcturus or Orion, Sun, and Aldebaran
Shimmering like leaves. I saw, not long ago,
A little girl close the door of her home in Nauvoo
And go to flowers she had planted by a spring.
The yellow and auburn of her dress, the white knots
In her braided hair, her eyes that kept their blue,
Despite the array they saw, seemed kept in light
In the afternoon. Her mother quietly followed her
To the fence and stood there watching: "Margaret,
You must leave them now. Put those in your hands
Aside and come with me." "Where, Mother?"
She asked, slowly turning. "We must leave
This home and find our way across the prairie
West." "Just across the river?" "Westward
Still, to a place called Laramie, and farther on,
Beyond the rising slope, to peaks and canyons
I have never seen." "Why?" she asked as soon
As she could lay her flowers beside the ones
That remained near the fence. "Because we believe."
"Mother, why do we believe as we do?" "Joseph
Came and talked to us about a harvesting."
"But Joseph is gone." "We believe as he believed.
Come. We must leave Nauvoo, and home, and find
Our way to Laramie." Later, on the prairie,
The girl and her mother walked together, the wagon
Ahead jostling through grass. Beyond, shadows
Of clouds spilled over a butte, and the red
Of its stone seemed leaden in hollow distances.
"Why do we believe as we do?" The girl dangled
A doll by the arm as she walked, believing

The prophecy of the city west in the mountains,
If not Zarahemla, Deseret, in the span
Of landfall east of the Sierra Nevada range
And the lake nearer still. I have heard
The whisper of the wagon wheels in the canyons,
The prophecy of wind over prairies, the cry
Of hosanna in the gray cirques of vision:
Home, the city is home, the slope of loam
And moraine against the cliffs, the twinkling
Of towns as the evening comes to Zion.
Time elides antiquity and the nearby years.
Margaret came with her doll in her arms,
Believing, and her great, great grandchildren
Gather their children around to tell how she
Came to the valley, stood on a hill to the east,
And cried her devotion.

THE PROFESSIONAL CHRISTIAN

Behold how Jesus fills my soul—
My friend, and savior of His Own.
I am One, and would make you:
Cleanse your wanton spirit's bole
As one would carve infected bone
Or bait and gouge a sacrificial Jew.
Come and know impeccably the Known.

I know the truth and speak for Him;
But illusion is the mask you wear,
An evil of our saeculum.
For you I hate—so crabbed, dim,
You whine as I demonstrate a flair,
Driving my doctrine and its inoculum
Behind your heretic eyes that wince and stare.

JESUS VAUDEVILLE FOR NEO–ROMANS

This sad-faced clown exaggerates his talent.
Sorrow, so arranged, especially with effects
Of streaks and tattered clothes, is in all respects
An acquired attitude. Should we help him? The salient
Term, humility, imposed or imposing, is either way
Rhetorical. See him wince his grief. How our anger
Rises that he does not make us laugh. His languor,
Hardly pure, was once assured in the ordinate play
Of a crucifixion. Those mechanistic Romans may
Have seemed efficient, but did not know their vaudeville.
We, much later, with varieties of performing skill,
Avail ourselves with flounce of lechery and stray,
Dissembled, into variations of theme, hardly knowing
The fiery seltzer that will rinse our menagerie away.
But still He writhes, beneficent and glowing
With an inner light, like porcelain.

TELEVISION EVANGELIST

Unbelievably benign, he knows you, reciprocal
As you watch and listen, ameliorative and quick
To Sunday lustre. Before him, you are slick
With caret dew that twinkles. The gospel call,
Included in his sentencing that is like a shawl
For one's indenturing, is lilt of curlew settling sick
Within his pining rhetoric. Verily, the trick
Is getting a flock to be as generative. The hall
Of his knowing is his mirroring. His cause
Is everything that anyone might gestate in him
And more (the gesture and the honied hymn
That belt his vaster audience with measure),
For what he knows he knows and says is pleasure
Unto him as, wonderfully, he mouths his gauze.

PRIME TIME PERSONAE
AT THIS POINT IN TIME

Siva, what do they have in common? A sacred cow
That they urgently entail to quash responsibility.
The jilts, so luminous in their dire nubility,
Try to score with verbiage to exhibit and endow
Their Presences with vaster clientele. To plow
It up and ply it is their endearment and civility;
They learned to deck you with it as a risibility
That gained a status, then two or three, as a way
To vacate mind. The gurus ply it too, certainly
Enough for one to excoriate them. Hair must lay
Against a temple to typify a scene so wantonly
An affront, though they may not sense it. A cay
Leeward of them will serve. To sit there for a day
To receive the belling wind! But who can dismay
These anchors who try to hook you on the news,
Or hang it in on you, as claque for all you know?
Siva, only you.

TELEVISION ANCHOR MAN

I am a stick on which to assemble clothes;
My flesh is air under pressure from the fan
Of my wavering verity. What I say in the van
Of my mind is presumption aerating into prose.
What presses my circumferences are the toes
Of my journalese in the sallow loam of pan-
Demic sense, that what I first wrote arose
From the paranatural, as if some demon chose
The void in which to cancel me. But who can
Do better than to lour verbatim of the street,
Not as humble deference but as supernal law
Which accretes into statement as a rickshaw
Of sticks to carry spines of the easy elite
On cobblestones of facts that hardly endure?
More than this is less than easy sinecure.

Still in the image of body is the shape of air
That rises afar, in eddies of the sun, as gold
Of spirit, as medallions of bronze in the fold
Of ships of the coast, where inlets are a lair
For prows that lift forward, where keels spare
Outward tumult of wake awash and white in cold
Marine that smoothed when the Holy Spirit told
Once helmsmen to sail under the rounding flare
Of seascape light. Where is the embodied Word
That walked on water in myths of eternal care?
But if it thrives, then I may languish, absurd
As I am with unholy opinion, billowing to bear
Gold templates of television though my clothes
Are rumply old, not a sail, nor petaling rose,
But empty as air.

HOT DOG

On the rise of snow and ice, he is magnificent.
Smooth of blue in nylon togs zipped at the seams,
He slips down a little run on skis and somehow reams
His calibre for us, who know him now as Millicent.
His haute couture, his musk, his dash, on his ascent,
Are freighted by an intramural dalliance of teams
Of snow bunnies with rouge and stick. Who deems
The sequitur? In boutiques he bellies up, so provident
To dispense his glory that we marvel at his expertise!
May he deign an Olympic run? The ninety-meter jump?
The giant slalom? The high-speed downhill? No.
He shows himself, his skill, his flourish in the sump
Of his grandeur. He cannot, will not, surely, row
The air, as he would have to, to get up speed.
He wends the slopes, exhibiting the very seed
Of pyrites, never gold, always such a tease.

FOREIGN MINISTER

Itchy coo. Mama's boy. Beddy-by-bye
Will be soon. Din-din's heavy on your tummy,
And, graying, you look bilious, not so sunny,
For this summitry and yet another try
At hemispheric peace. But how could anyone try
To figure you? So old, you seem a comic, funny
On such occasions. You shuffle cue cards, rummy,
Tipsy-turvy with legality. One should not pry
Into why you cavil and bluster, paranoid,
To get your way, giving not a graying inch.
The world should wise up, count you null and void.
But shifty you, you move technically like a winch
To haul yourself upstage. Your expertise you sell
As vital to the issue, whether a ne'er-do-well
Or not, I'm sure.

MERIT PAY INCREASE

Incredibly, it began in the minds of the risible,
Wonderfully interesting in that a singular persona
Might consider himself the primum mobile in the corona
Of his own enlightenment. Was he, is he responsible
For the vacuity of the System? And is it defensible
If it cannot be seen or touched? Verily, he has flown
In a vacuity whose essence is the aether acetone.
His ounce of energy deliquesces, generally visible
As a hue in the vivid fever of his own accountancy.
The rock of his salvation is the nada of reference
That thins, abstracted in the clear effervescence
Of fluorine in the world of works, whose constancy
Transmogrifies what everyone thinks someone knows.
But this someone squats in it to judge whatever shows
As ragweed, silkworm, tatter, or rime of Calliope.

PROLOGUE TO A GERIATRIC HONOR
FOR FORTY YEARS OF TEACHING

An honor for the precise yield of knowledge,
Or is it a token for which all else is handy,
Echo of lyric or hushing pledge
To stick to the word like meaning? The sandy
Years flow, impressionable as vellum to ink,
Golden, and disappear. He would teach,
From the word hoard, freshmen, in themes
Of affection, English, parenthetic to reach
The environment of sense in the skiving dreams
Of meaning. He likes to think his honor is
Glistening of words, poetry, and the discursive pen
Easily moving. He is humble (but higher than Dis),
Especially with books whose visionary ken
Lifts the vision like Barbara's from a leaf,
Iridescing in belief.

GALLERY ON THE EIGHTEENTH GREEN

They murmur the cadences of their devotion,
Consecrated in purpose as in faith:
Still, still in the silence, in the motion
Of winds, in the shade, the wraith
Of holy excellence settles here, faint with emotion.

WHAT DOES ONE KNOW

About the Civil War? Though long forgotten,
It provides a discipline that crafts the mind.
Fingers stroke the thinnest swaths that bind
The mythic sense that is chambered in cotton
Or in tapestry that blackens into sandy soil.
Memory may loft away into clerestory light,
But war is kept as pain is kept, compressed
In a jacket that is bound behind. Far West,
Into western light, a swallow that is bright
And well configured dips and skims to assess
This shade. It is low as a grave in a hook
Of stone. The ache of knowing of it is less
Than that reality, like the rumple in a book
Of ribs along a ditch or a thorax in a mess
Of uniform and iron gear. Forget and chess

For comfort. How can anyone learn or know?
Lincoln, at some windy helm, looked stonily
At war and wept. If only, and if just bonily,
A spectre would reach out and shift a row
Of soldiery to meet the enemy in their repose,
If only materiel were there, in its place,
With which to secure a gain on land! A trace
Of some remembrance in death's face shows
Itself, intermittently, as a hallowing of eyes
Against a wall. Close down the multi-thousand
Casualties against themselves, who shall rise
As wraiths that cannot live again, whose sand
Of graves shifts in time of war. Keep the prize
Of living now, and from war's darkness strive

Into the air to breathe before you know.

GENERAL MEADE OF GETTYSBURG

Why am I the army's command? And here? The field
Trespasses into the sky, and trees, in the railing
Light, move as if shaken from below. The tides
Of armament rise along a perimeter. Lincoln,
Of official Washington, sets my will to stay
And field the revulsion of calm. A bugle cries
The solemnity of charge, and tight stars of rank
Revive my bearing into a rod of the mind's alignment.
Look! Brevet Custer wheels left against a hill.
Stannard levels his cannon. Hancock braces
In a chamber of trees. Fires of light intercede,
Driving through smoke. In the cleft of a devil's den
A rift appears. Rows and rows of Carolingians
Pitch and fall graciously to smolder in halls
Of lesser vision. Soldiery march sunlit and drawn
As in a sketch for a daguerreotype in the seethe
Of a thundercloud gathering heat and rolling.
The mounted slip askew, failing from sabres
That rise and sparkle where underlings thresh
And wind in unison. The grille of white smoke
Keeps apertures of fire that reverberate
The sounds of powdering. Why am I here in turn,
A way of being in command in avenues of holiness,
Fevering into decisions to hold here and there
Along the line? Christianly, I yield myself
Near the rock of an angle, caisson in the rustling field,
And the cannister that puffs away, emblazoning
The shadows of my humility before the prince
Of generals on his white mount, pointing here.
I stay. I pitch and hold against his command.
I stay because the field is Gettysburg in the ring
And cavalry of Lincoln's wish, gripped as reins
Are gripped and steadied. I am the horseman with a scythe
That holds the dead that become the dead I touch
In my marrow, in the dials of silence, and in flares

That steal into the dark of my eyes. I worship
The leaping crown fire as it draws my soldiery
To mass and hold in Lincoln's vivid resolution.

SHENANDOAH

The blue ridge remains as dark as evening
In the afterglow. The gray line vanishes
North into pallor where mist vanquishes
The memory of Antietam Creek. The leavening
Of history is like a drift of snow ravening
Light that must remain to shine. Who languishes
In a creek, aglow, reddening, as his wishes
Calm themselves into tears? Convening
Blood, ardent across the sodden wool
Of his bivouac, is crumpled still, unresponding
To the heaving twist of reaching down into the pooling
Rill where his feet remain. Generalissimo, full
Of salients of secession, coordinate
The sweep and thrust of columns as, inebriate
With advantage, you seek out Gettysburg.

READING SPENSER

Spenser, prince of the Renaissance, you kept
Your fealty like samite in strands of imagery
That fall from stanzas in the richest vagary
Of discipline. You are the prince yclept
Magnificence who holds the flower that slept
The ages of wonder in the spell, or perjury,
Of someone such as Colin or sylvan Margery.
Once again from their bower they have crept
To test the meadow for its dew, the song
Of nightingales, the flowering of vales
Of light. And if you should come, a throng
Like them behind you, following . . . What pales
Before me? Never my knowing that in your will
The Word shall live, that you are living still.

COLERIDGE

The pyre of stars midair, the slope of vision,
And language as easy as nap caressed
By the hand of light. The ship of sails
Reaches the margent dusk: dusk near Bristol
And the channel of sea. There, on the bank,
He sits, with a blue lotus of Vishnu nearby.
The span of wings overhead, and the Southern Cross
Rises from the southern horizon, the sea that weighs
Heavily upon the round of earth below its curve.
These are your notes, Coleridge—images of person
In the relative continuum of space and time
A hundred years before it was pronounced as theory.
Why not receive the images that enrich the spectrum
Of violet into visions of energy across the sky,
As the southern sky dawns for you?

T. S. ELIOT

The anguish of the years he spent alone
Beside the tumid river of the mind:
The waste land increate: the roses bind
The slightest movement of the chirping bone.
What was the final thing the old guy said?
Ah, yes, "The horror! The horror!" Not the name
By which he tinkers endlessly with shame—
That cockle-warming word was always dead.

Sterile conversion comes, beneath a tree;
The bone has faith, relishes its white,
Exults in finding for itself reprieve
From gritting winds that wander, dry and free.
Discovery comes, confronted by the night:
The better thing to do is to believe.

EVENING: TO JOHN MILTON

Never have you seen him, but he remembers
The dark surface of your sleep that like a leaf
Lies still on a pavilion of water. In the grief
Of Gethsemane, he glances as if in a dream
Of centuries that break into surf as they teem
With morning: yellow gold, blue of azure, reef
Of sun, goldstone, crystal cave, windsor sheaf
Of amber, tourmaline, diamond, and starry stream.
More godly is communion's skiey censer wafting
Cloudy vales where the wind's winnowing is repose!
He can be seen in the far canebrake, on rafting
Light of the lake where the arc of day glows
Into silk, then at evening, but never so much
As in the hint of dawn at evening, his lightest touch.

FUN HOUSE MANIKIN

The imperishable megaphone rollicks,
Hilarious in forty-second tours.
She shakes, the weighty rustic shakes,
A manikin spotted and obscene,
Palms out, paunch shuddering,
Mouth triple-toothed and open black.
Thus she plays charades of happiness.
Worry for her, broadcloth, wire, and plastic,
Ever there, ever there, flapping out
And endlessly insane.

SKYSCRAPER

Man is made in Eden again,
From sin
And a snake babbling malice
To murder his heel.

At last knowing the finesse of our mode
Of knowing
I know the tower Babel built to God:
But the reach offends like the mad paw of the cheetah
Moving black and like a dazzling wing.

At the waterfront in Chicago,
By the museum and the great hotel,
The intent grows preposterous:
The rivets burn and cool;
The girders vault, encased in artificial stone;
The lines converge from bases mountainous to infinity,
High as Denver in the West—

Tier on tier of glass amazing
The whimsical and floating clouds,
Airy as they,
There like the pavilions of stars,
Or all that God walks on,
The flashings and the structure of light.

ASCENT FROM A DIVIDER

[See commentary]

As if hollow ground as a knife may be, the divider
On the interstate stiffens this variety's market
Of hot, rousting cars in narrow lanes like a carpet
Rousingly undulant, and my mind, like an outrider,
Divines the madness of its consistency. I fire
The atmosphere, throttling, as it exsufflicates
Gaslight carbons of petroleum and exacerbates
The slipstream glare. There, instantly, a tire
Mark on the divider, ecstatically aplomb, suggests
Parabola. How could rack and pinion put it there
But from severe angulation of chassis and frame
Across the lanes, splitting airborne, rattling fame
Of chrome, engine oil stippling through the tests
Of torque, then there, easily ascending, dissolving
Into antecedents of terror, to die forensic, revolving
In the sky, to be metalled in a Bessemer of sun?

SEVEN–TENTHS OF A SECOND
[See commentary]

There's the tree, shaded and stolid as death,
And you, in the impress of speed, a mile a minute
On a register, weigh forward with your last breath
To note in a curious gravity the casual limit

Of an illusion pressing you to settle still
Forward at three thousand, two hundred pounds.
In the compression the bumper flows into the grill,
And its bits of steel slip into the tree with sounds

Of puncturing; the hood rises and waves into the shield
In front of you as the drive of wheels lifts and hovers,
Twisting openly; the grill spills its flakes, annealed
Into colors of light; the body steel covers

The trunk as if a casual mantle sloping in
And corresponding; and the rear enfolds and splays
The doors that move like tongues floating in
A discourse of the day. Your body plays

Against its speed as the structures near you
Brake you easily: your legs reach straight,
Snap at the knees, leaping short, and shear you
At the groin; off the seat, your torso like a crate

Settles into the dashboard as your chest and arm
Curve the steering wheel; you crest into the visor,
Though you cannot see the pitching motor block harm
The chipping trunk, for you keep speed, wiser

Than before without knowing; the steering column
Bends vertical, and you, driven and impaled,
Fail inwardly, pulsing blood into your solemn
Lungs. Your head is mantled and assailed

With glass. The car reclines into the ground,
Conforming noisily as hinges rip, doors pry
And rail the air, and seats rise, puff, and bound
Forward to press and pin you where you die.

MACHINE PRESS

The cast steel trundles on rollers over the floor,
Heads and gears and blocks, the instrumented
And casual weight that rumbles like war.
Subtly heaving, it turns under chains regimented
As tackle by pulleys and the spring of steel.
The machinist, in his careful scrutiny,
Shifts the weight, smoothly turns a wheel,
Pushes and glides, eventual as destiny,
Careful as God with the impress of pain,
And swings with it in the magnificent air
Because he holds it stilling there.

Then he turns to the ritual of the press
In a reverie for some mettle of devotion
And opens it, by a handle raising it less
As a matter of fear than of competent motion.
A myriad times before in the grave
Towers of precision he had judged his surety,
Had vacated chance with a wave
Of concern and rational purity,
Had, in his wisdom, wielded his fright,
Had willed what he knew until it was trite.

Then some slip of oil gleaming on the floor,
The thrust under, the jostling weight
Incalculable and wandering, and the shore
Of precision, where? His palms near the plate
Of his sacrifice, the handle and descending forge
Press his thumbs and index fingers paper thin
That will not grasp the even world again.

ROCKET SLED

Judge from here, the dais, chair, the square
And stately place on rails:
Then the tubular, matched ignition,
The puff, the shot of power,
And the dour jowls.
Ah, the age of speed becomes thee!
The court you quickly hold against the
Still air ripples your skin like sails
And yawns beneath your rocks of eyes
Some question of the pushing fire
Until a fin settles in a water trough
And brakes you like a jockey on a mule.
What an upright, square, impossible chair
You hold, so seriously a judge of what we are,
You Calvinist latched before the sovereign clouds
Of alcohol and liquid air!

EXECUTION OF THE INNOCENTS

Let us begin with the benign anonymity
That encrusts awareness. Any tantamount
Of innocents will serve, wherever the fount
Of ingenuity spurges tears in the unanimity
Of recollection. Smalling, their sanity
Eminent, they cannot savor thought, are not wont
To think less of the cunning cadre they daunt
With winsome and ingenuous smiles. The vanity
Of those who wield our cordite is not in question.
They who lour, sage with inevitable will, seize
The straw of resolution, venerable in the lees
Of gearing dialectic. Grey in the stanchion
Of light overcasting them, they filter desire.
One now titters a pleasantry, coddling fire

That punctures her temple, surreptitiously shattering
Bone into the recesses of her kindly intuition.
Another, fancifully dressed for the day's diminution
Of her genealogy, is not aware of the pattering
Of rain that divests the sun amid scattering
Shot. What erupts but her red spume? Revolution
Is an act of earth, change the unruly fission
Of life undersea, dialectic the immense chattering
Of the mammalians of gusty politics that emerge
Into yet a higher order. No matter the innocence,
The eyes adew, the sniffling near the demiurge
Of his revolt. The systemic, psychopathic urge
To choose determines their execution, from whence
Proceedeth sense of dominance, when to purge

As one might choose emetic for any viral
Insurgency. Monarchs failed, their children sweet
Beside them, under them, as, quickly, the elite
Also died. House or genera must fail, mural
Of their photogenesis, as in a frame. Coral

Dies into remembrance, glistening where to steep
The sea aglow with white and pink. The heap
Of this decay, as in a sty, cannot survive. The feral
Beauty is a daguerreotype to be remembered as forlorn.
They had to die, with whatever concocted evidence.
Nicholas, Alexandra, and their little ones were shorn
Of their cashmere of hauteur. Red banners flutter hence,
Then the hammer and sickle as the dire horsemen sense
The vertigo of their opportunity. Who can forget
The vast communal expiation of the red regret?

FOOTBALL GAME

The announcer's voice weighs forward, grave
With import and evidence. But what transpires?
Knuckles loosen, jerking; a groin cracks;
A tendon rips away; redundant racks
Of teeth lean; noses smear; leading wires
Of mind jostle, thrumming in a case; pyres
Of pain spurt and char; a leg lacks
Resilience, breaks; eyes behold tacks
Of consciousness in day's vivid gyres
Of the Valkyrie; a skeleton rummages, stiff
Through itself, hunching; hernia and cartilage
Pop against a drum of air; and a midriff
Fails as the announcer indulges in persiflage
And notes coincidence. Guard and tackle sack,
Hang, and draw the quarterback. Offsides.
Call it all back and do it again.

PAC MAN: AN ENORMITY?

Disembodied omnivore, your head is a perfect round
But for your mouth, by which you find direction
To edibles nourishing nothing in your defection
From whatever body that ever is. But you abound,
In current lore, in a career that must astound
To satisfy. Consuming everything in your election
In the mind of man, you satisfy a yen for insurrection
That he has hidden in his animus. So he is bound
To play his nature out, erecting electrostatic gear
To keep resplendent in a light of mind that glows
Across the widening empyrean of his subtle fear
That he mirrors an omnipotence that always knows.
Consider yourself intrinsically. You're not so shoddy;
You clear all capillaries like an antibody.

GENETIC LIMITATION

The hawk and greyhound can see illimitably;
The hummingbird can fix a place in flight
And sip from it; the redbreast can hear aright
Where the stir is, underground. Indubitably,
A body's gift is precise, as is, inimitably,
That of the cow drenched in mercurial fright
Of the packer's stall. We judge her mildly trite
As a strolling factory that waits immitigably
To be split beef hanging from a hook in a cape
Of frost. You see her eyes garishly protrude
Askance and stare wildly away to find escape
Where it never is. Variously wrapped as food,
She figures among items for the worming tape
Of our advantage. But what are the subtler gifts
That we exploit, usurping Anubis where he sifts,
Dispiriting?

HYPE

But how could it exquisitely
Float away lighter than air, tied to inveterate
Lead? That lead shall never be more than it is,
Soft to any knife and always the same,
Some slight lustre almost silvery, but in any
Alloy deadly, or in a spray of fluorescence.
Do not breathe around it, as it is available.
The synchrony begins. The balloon incredibly
Becomes rotund past all believing, a gaseous marvel
That seems to nod. And someone has woven
The string into a sheathing cable! O Transamerica!
It is heavenly now, skiey like all else
Determined to succeed, and through the sheer presence
Of all it seems to be I may believe, consonant
Between my eyes and handled again and again.
It is mine and I
Until balloon is all that I shall try to be forever
As a stint for health, aided to my shekels by the measureless mass
That has seen it too. Lead transcending,
Resurrected, wobbling up, asteroid supervening
Into star and superstar.

LIQUID PAPER

The paper was crinkly and translucent as India.
I put it into the typewriter, deftly straightening
An edge to a sighting line, flipped a lever,
And was off into letters. But now "facilite,"
An "e" in error, but perhaps not an error—
Rather, French from wishful thinking. No way
To let it be, not even as an irony. Oh, now,
A swish of liquid paper, drying, on which
To type precision and perfection, as if
The error was never there to be redeemed,
I smooth the error white and turn the phrase,
So nicely corrigible, into virtue's "facility
Of light," in lightest conjuring. And then away,
As if the paper were waterleaf where myth
Resides, the flowing ease that rises inwardly,
Welling softly into being.

RACISM

Protean permutations provide skins that cause
The brow to knit a wool and agitate the Law
To achieve a justice that like a genetic taw
Moves into social light only now to pause
For our beholding. Who is this who gnaws
At the gate of equality? There, the maw
Of Cerberus opens, carking that the flaw
That Cause bestowed is with us yet and straws
Our most discerning thinking. Vivid difference
Is the issue, the not-like-me a mean advantage
That rises in the gorge like the prurience
Of one's identity. I AM is the cause of rage,
And roasting heterodoxy his disunion in the mind
Of the unisectarian who must taste his rind.

EXTRATERRESTRIAL

That clouded blue recedes
As a port for astronauts,
And now sills of moon
Appear as the spacecraft
Smooths over into orbit.
Far away, a shaft
Of dusty light slips down
Upon concentric spots
Of sun that cloud
Into fields of Saturn.
And then away, the craft
Vanishing in its trajectory
Toward gorgeous Aldebaran
As Jehovah rides a sunstream,
Slumming for the second time to get
What He has coming.

IT WILL NOT SELL

"No, it will not sell," he seethed. "No way.
And even if, with subsidy, it did, we would take
Or rake in more than half the gross. Morgan le Fay
Could do no better, or even some fabled sheik
Riding the carpet of Allah to bequeath the golden
Coins of Caesar would not sponsor or embolden
You."

In through the walls of glass and ceramic tile
I go, as if the foyer were a heaven's windrow mile.
If I were tiny Thumb, the carpet would seem
A field of wheat in the silent air, or a stream
If over it the wind would pass, or seraphim.
In that sepulchral quietness, where cherubim
Glow just beyond the starlight pendentine,
Blue vistas of the evening deepen into indigo.
And there, unbending from a desk, a pale imago
Greets me, soft of tone, solicitous, inquiring,
"What can I do for you?" And I, fully desiring
Expedience to prolong this sensuous diversion
Into ambiance, reply, "I am, on this excursion,
Quite overcome. But may I see the lofty manager
Or the editor-in-chief?" She moves, as if a tanager
From limb to limb, and asks, "Is this the hour
For you, and the day?" "Yes," I aver, and lour
To see her eyebrows still. "Is something wrong?"
I breathe. "No," she replies, "but don't be long.
His mood is delicate." So hovering down a hall
In a minor ecstasy, I anticipate the easy fall
Of wisdom from his empyrean, so prim and prime
Myself like any elf pursing to the tart lime
Of his greenery. The carpet is very citric too,
Matching the panels of upholstery and the couch
On which I sit, and sink, as if it were a pouch
Or a velvet coach of the decorous Louis Quinze,

Who, lazily encumbered by his wigs and fans,
Bravely flourished. Might I surreptitiously escape,
Tumbling down the stairs, or sullenly traipse
Away to swing from candelabras, out of here?
But, seeing a welling tear, I still, amazed.
It matters little that acres here were razed
To house him. He says, "I sense your cause
And, remembering, savor the anthology of verse
You sent me weeks ago." "Yes," I say, perverse
And staring as I sense occlusion. "I pause
To say that angels wait on you, not knowing whether
To abandon finest hope or, sallowing like leather,
To sicken slowly, wavering." He says, "How forlorn
Of you to think that we might this or any day elicit
Policy from our editorial board to hem the deficit
That publishing this verse would certainly incur."
Then on my back I feel the fuzz that turns to fur
As I inwardly sense in him the gleaming wolverine.

VANESSA DOES HER MOVIE "PLAYING FOR TIME"

Anti-Zionist claque preens terrorism for the PLO;
The PLO vends bombs at Kennedy Airport: Auschwitz
The camp remains, where the four million infuse
Terrain, ash from smoke to fertilize the greenery
As photogenesis corrects impressions of holocaust.
Vanessa acts the victim who sang "Madame Butterfly"
In sympathy for the downcast victims of the world,
Creating dramatic ironies and tension out of story,
Umbrage in any discrete Jew notwithstanding. For all
Is sentiment in her, to be used broadly to augment
The vision of film's illusion. She is veritable Cadillac
Idling for film, eructable, but artist of resolution
Of spirit, her delusion restricting like pens of wire,
The ultimate fake of movie queen made out to be sincere.
Her sackcloth is for tears, her makeup for the whited
Miller. Such anguish for children pitched into graves
To writhe before cleats of SS generals who mince
Delights to rhythms of a train, the hissing lights,
And puffing chemicals! After a scene, Vanessa adjusts
Her conscience: anarchist Vanessa, Palestinian,
Will play, for Yasser, victim Jewess, as actress
Milling among the stripping chains of wire
For Jews who die, sweet sentiment upon her lips
To be savored, pearling into monologue of virgin
Sociology.

TERRORIST

Her arms trembled like tatters in windrow trees,
But the wind of that terror cannot stir the mould
Of her flesh that falls against stone, as in a frieze.

See, the flesh of her face slopes in a mirage
Of heat, surreal. So I fan the radiances
That blend into lava, becoming the phage

That invades the dimming sun as the lustre
Of gold, weathering time. She screamed at dolls
Before her—not dolls, but as strewn, muster

Forgotten where they lay, resting in a frenzy
Of clothing, rumpled as old bedding, driven
Down into silence, throats open to the quinsy

Of death, the foetor. She was roused and taken
In the canvass of homes, marched with bayonets
To a compound of glinting wire, and there forsaken.

Mother of sons, I remember you alone from them,
And I alone remain as the hand thick with resin
That seizes Day. You were taken, your hem

Raised as a banner. The lights of my mind
Sparkle, decisive, to measure the possibility
Of the box of the pale apocalypse I find

To wield, with wires and fasces of plasm.
To wings of the heaven I rise, in a cockpit
Commanding my agency over a chasm

Of air and widening power. Mother, you came
Spiralling in a dream, tatters of arms, crying,
And I murmur your cause and your dead name

As I write with the wand of justice a stewardess
Sees. Her eyes widen into mine, seeing.
She sways in an amber beam, in the stress

Of her poise. A voice in the air blessing
All cordite revives the liturgy of her oblivion
As I receive the nestling from your shawl, caressing

Its power. This is the ark of my devotion.
Its relic dwells for me, and its silver sheen
Must stir like the snail of my dim revulsion.

I do not fail. I am the god of the weeping
I feel in the anguish of your beholding eyes.
From the final charisma of passengers a seeping

Terror surprises me. Now. Algiers of the twilight
East. Like the stinging wire of a garroting,
I tighten easily as my wreathing insight

Bequeaths the Enemy.

NUCLEAR WINTER

The myrtle falls across the wall,
And the evening's darkness, like a shawl,
　　Wraps the light and holds it in,
After the firewinds of Fall.

Though sun will come, it withers fast,
Crumbling leaves as if the past
　　Had not been, and did not teem,
As if it was not meant to last

Beyond an image in the holy mind,
As if not meant to shape the wind
　　To wend around the rosy sun
Of flowering, nor quietly to find

A place of evergreen to flourish in.
The newer winter has come to spin
　　The sun around, and never warm.
The air is dry, and human skin

Crisps in nitrogen.

THE CLOSING IRIS OF ESCAPE, 2531 A.D.

Since the storm of methane over the char
And ice, I have kept our records as I do now.
Once vision was of the heavens, what mind will allow,
Horizon to horizon the fullest aperture, the quick car
Of our transport in the illimitable hush, far
Light of the sun a twinkle in nigre, how
We see to return to the blue pale of the Thou
Of our kept religion. This, then, is the mar
Of our plan, the spheroid weight of a zero.
We might have returned, and yet may, or not,
But the heavens are now the ever placid night,
Strangely an iris closing, improbably wrought
In desire and guess. The once irruption, slight
As we felt it, tilted us into an impossible lie,
To an angle badly and lowly depressed. The dry

Cold absorbs our last power as a needle reads
Down into loss. The iris of meaning scans
Subtly to array our science. The white fans
Of dust still overhead. Very soon, someone pleads
In a murmur, breathless. This, simply, among needs:
Only a chance to return. The commander nods, as he plans
The touch of Greenwich time, and lists, when he spans
Trajectory, to peer into space. Too slow, in the weeds
Of our sorrow, too low to return to the higher curve
That may bring us in. Even so, we will softly glide
Down and away, lost in unavailing silence, to swerve
Into gravities of light, away into the loss we deride
With tongues of our silence the incalculable disaster
Of accidence through distances we never could master.

QUIRKY QUARKS

[See commentary]

From Uhuru . * o O quarking con flu of erg
Out updownwhen inout Oh O E=mc² ad hoc
Roundingup inround sphering tic tick tock
Rousing McReisenstein's carrousel of Stellaberg
And moraine overunbending the cirque's spurge
Of teensy quarks vanishing into being un loc
Cit closing out in the primeval coeval shock
Of power in the infinitesimal balk urge
Of a galactic swish hardlea into the event
Horizon of the unified unfielding universe,
And One will admit in the bower of terse
Statement nothing plus all for the inverse
Of expansion in Shakespeare's Hamlet anent
A reform, an eutron star black to farrow
Another euiniverse chuffing in all respecks
. *)=(+ even for us the water crystalline +

THE THEORY OF RELATIVITY

Understand that, vis-à-vis experience,
Any understanding is only relative,
A point of view. Outrage, expletive,
Or question cannot void in the Omniscience
That sequesters the small insouciance
That afflicts us all. Become contemplative.
Distill all you know into an aperitif
To be quaffed meretriciously in the skiff
Of a final sundown that may be tentative.
You cannot understand accreting evidence.
It rests forever in the mystic providence
Of aery eiderdown or, perhaps, in a dense
Field of nuclei compressed into round
Or purée of gravity. And this is stock
Accountancy only now, like smalling talk
That we enjoin to suppress our prescience
That Relativity is relative only to Light.

EINSTEIN

In the fold of time Elohim the King strides
Into the space of his creation as he elides
Its limit, or the ending. Arcturus clamors
Windsong, nearly tinkling, as the sun abides

Dark amid dust, barely seen. And now the cycle
Of his circumambience, once again a circle
Shaping, as he rounds the universe and defines
Its size in circumferences of speed that trickle

Into intimation. O swift that wavers on a limb,
Arise; the silver lilac is near, the diadem a dim circlet of sun
Vanishing quite away, for day
Is gone, and you alone must ride at dusk the slim
Ray that may arrive in me from his declension,
Insilvering. The swell of gravity in the gentian sepulchre or
Precipitate speed is an image
Drawn from eternity, the edge of our invention.

VIRGO OF THE THOUSAND GALAXIES

Who has not seen the imperial sun
Flash into the steadiness of splendor,
Green and cerise, emerald and pink,
Resounding down the clarion brink
Of the interstellar light where the vendor
Of truth reigns, freely and silently undone

As a gift of rendering in a vale of embers?
For this is the nearer sun in its repose
In the midway of Orion. Where may it flash
In the clouds of darkness? Where may it trash
The beads of glimmering into the rose
Of larger fire, weathering? Who remembers

The tetrahelion of orbits to venerate
Another order drawn into the press of gravity
To achieve the singular? Vision lies in a petal
Against the similar light that made it from metal
Drifting down from the broken stars in a depravity
Of dissimulation. We are as necessary, elate

To see it, narrowing into the span of fire
And time in the wisping of the final voyager.
We are as close as diatoms that laze
In their concentricity. See and praise
The full event, the trillion quantum integer
Of the unity that is the final pyre:

Virgo of the suns of galaxies, burning like a bush.

A CHILDISH FASCINATION WITH STARS

Forget the vertigo of pain. In that starry cache
Is the vast continuum of nuclear fusion. Our task
Is to learn about it. Not all ignition in its masque
Of violence is the consequence of mass and the lash
Of gravity. Many, or most, must happen amid trash
Of humanoid psychoses, in some either/or wisk
Of political decision wafting a very hot disc
Of light. Ah, see at their height missiles flash
As a humanoid quirk! A pulse of ten million degrees
At its arcing source that ignites a rod of plutonium!
See it burst. See how its rolling blast, in the lees
Of power, consumes the crisps of our continuum,
Our circles of ash wisping into vast circles of fire.
This is the way. We adore the universal pyre.

THE TWIN PLANETS
[See commentary]

Consider that figment called the moon.
Catheter of any wild guess, it stares,
The sordid real: darkness and the sun
Abrade with cold and heat and only crack
The rock, the extrinsic chip, pocketed and pale,
The leper twin of earth. It stares, long dead
And steady as its death's head mockery.
                    But valleys
Where the seas should be gaze emptily
Their impotence to generate or aid
A single juvenescent spore. Incessant
Rock wanders with its ceaseless rolling
In our balding scrutiny, and we lace our minds
With honey from the smalling bees that buzz
Enchantment that we may know enough to offset
God and put Him off as prettily as a child
Begging to recite some lisping Pentateuch.
                    You cannot
Put Him off. He hangs hell beyond our air
And shows Himself to us as creator of titanic opposites,
For us the filament of green bending lightly
In the shade or in the warmth of sun.

THE DARK PLANET: A PROSPECT OF THE END
[See commentary]

The firmament responded to a bath
Of photographic salts, and showed itself,
A negative, as blackish periods,
As if to be the end of all the Words
Pronounced by God across the edge of time
As if to say no consequence again,
Another portrait of the firmament —
No consequence, no consequence, a map
Of nebulae and supernovae bursting
From the center of the universe
In slowly boiling light and cosmic dust,
Concentric rings and wispy spirals flat
In space, that hurtle to the deeper void
At speeds, according to the calculations
Based on readings of the spectral red,
Expressed by zeros, multitudinous
And uniform, adjacent to the numbers
On their left, in pretty groups of three.

The universe explodes and all is calm—
Except a blur of black across a corner
Of the plate, so trivial and near.
Now palsy, of the rudest sort, disrupting
Equanimity: the twitching questions
Check the telescope and fumble dials
Corroborating now the wispy path,
Coincident with earth's within the void.
The pallid fingernails appoint the time
On pads of paper near the telescope,
Now synchronized upon the orbing blur
As bright as Mars, but thriving like a mold,
Benign, upon the photographic plates.
The information slips beyond the doors
And leaps along the catenary wires

That undulate across the countryside:
The prescience, the prescience of death
That dresses the tongue with lye and felt
Or stalks along the parapets and towers,
Invisible and lithe, astride the world;
The instant scream, the black and gaping circle
Sinking through the marrow of the spine.
The hours disappear, congealed on windows
Mordant with the light of afternoon . . .

Another night, as silence leaps from eye
To eye, discordant with the tiny moon
That slices optic paths with slivers
Of its light; the planet hurtles, boring
With the anguish of Gethsemane,
Embellished with its pinnacles of thorns.
And here the archway of the calla lilies
Palms and candelabra; here the woman,
Her escort rigid in grimace and tails:
A gown of satin, covered with a yoke
Of lace, its full-hooped skirt in swirls
That fall into a court-length train, a veil
Of laced illusion, trimmed with seed pearls sewn
Along the stems of split carnations,
Petrified in simulated coruscations,
Fettered by a white tiara's grasp.
The hours settle with the stamen dust
Upon the surfaces of hardwood floors
That flicker in the light of afternoon
And glaze the lashes of the mannequin.

The speechless speak, their words exorbitant
And wan, encumbered by the prophecies
That hurtle from the edge of Babylon.

The hours roll—collision minus ten,
And death a wispy crescent couched in stars. . . .

The wakeless dead are numb with fettered grief
That reaches only to the living loam;
Upon the earth the rigor of the grave,
As seconds, minutes abrade the lilies thin
And tombstones, multitudinous, agape,
Disdain the waving, tipping stems
Affrighted by paralysis and awe.
The planet seems to hover like the moon,
Its cragged surface scourged and terrible;
The planet comes, collision minus one,
At twilight, with the evening star,
Rumbling with the tides of gravity
That grasp and roll its vast circumference.
And less the time, and less: the massive ball
Impales the sky and atmosphere,
The tearing rush at earth—mountains split
And valleys crackle in titanic storms.
O Lord, horizons fold before its fire!

THE UNIFIED FIELD

An endless line cast to a curve in the pearling dark
Allows the universal light. They, wending together,
Found and are divinity. All turning is eternity, stark
Vacuum of nothing but the echo or the gusting heather
Of energy. There, beyond, is the mind's fine tether
That we cannot drop abroad in a meadow where a lark
Rises to warble and trill. We cast our linear wishing
Along the imperial curve, but straighten it to fit
Lines of the parallax whose points are the nearby sun
Of our envisioning. If the two become one, swishing
The void and starring it, they are the endless One,
Infinitesimally then drawn into the infinite heat,
The circling Alpha and Omega, the decimal One.

PARABLE

The fibres of evening burn eternally,
The wick of God whose energy is hydrogen
Fuming at twenty million degrees
In that cause of light, the sun.
Ah, Saviour, teach me warmth
And gravity through the gentle epithet
In the sentimental glow of twilight,
In the song of your speech,
Easement of the infinite fire.

FINAL DECISION

"What shall it be, fission or fusion?"
"Not fission. There's too much of that
Already. This falling apart pitter-pat
And wily-nily only adds to the confusion."

"The fusion of the median sun's revising
Hydrogen into helium is certainly a flash
Of the Alpha fire. Ah, let us trash
This earth of our unique devising,

Clearly once like Eden." "The paradisal
Glass from silicon must quickly fuse
For its ending. Therefore, let man abuse
His platelets of plasm as our reprisal

For his many sins." "So well instructed,
How could he, though finicking and amiss,
Confuse himself in preternatural bliss
Like Arthur Pendragon, whom we inducted

As a modern prince into magnificence,
Who fell into straits of complication
When Guinevere, in her convocation
With a paramour, exhibited less sense

Than Eve?" "Well, surely this is enough—
This hot emulation of the origin and cause."
And so They pause and think and pause
Before the cataclysm in which they sough

Our red giant sun across the frosty peaks
That touch into flame. Revere the flowing
Stone and magma sintering as we flare, lowing
In our immolation, into streaks

Of God's fiery sarabande.

ALPHA AND OMEGA AT THE END

This dream, arising from a cloud of seeming,
Is a sea of glass that first in fusion
Formed from the pyre of a once delusion,
Siftings of earth and sky, and of dreaming,
Quite near in fond regularity as a reliquary
Of early history. The crane of imperial light
Seized the light and cast it high as yearning
That stopped at the precipice and the ferning
Uplands of sintering magma and labradorite,
Nestling in gemming nitre, carbon, and feldspar
Into pools of the Unified Field. But you might bar
The real, or disclose it. See the encumbering star
That will fail as others did, and this that warms us
Is memory, but the soul's retention harms us

If we think that aught might remain. What remains,
In my candor, is the illusion that out there
Can be recorded and kept in an error called here,
Or within. Within the fragment of was, stains
The solipsism. I am the bridge, not the land
Or a shore, but a bridge with no end of passing,
Air to air, space to space, no stream, but the massing
Of the diaphane, the pavane, and the incredible sand
Washed into the luminous sea of glass, in fire.
Fond illusion, you persist in me as I tire,
For I am your memory, your faith in the first spire,
Rustling through me as memory, the aery lyre,
And my song. I gather you in at a balustrade
Of sapphire, and begin again as Alpha and Aubade.

ADONOI OF THE CREATION
[See commentary]

One must nurture a seedling into its compleat compaction
Singularly and vastly hot at 10^{-43} second at trillions
Of degrees centigrade, burgeoning at 10^{23}K, vermilions
In blue, white, black, and infrared in a refraction
Of brown, yellow, and green, and the universe of our sanction
At this point is but a mote of 10^{-28} centimeter in a pylon
Of force irradiating into an inflationary epoch like nylon
In strands and tides to 10^{-24} cm, now cooling in reaction
To its Unified Field, now sundering into exponentiality
But reheating into identities of the ingenious veniality
Of quarks, electrons, and mirror images of the traction
Of antimatter against matter: as, for example, the interaction
Of electrons with positrons into a suburban annihilation
Of all but a little matter, about the size of an elation
Of egg. Ah, this omelet grilling at 10^{-32}, a mere tick,
At 10^{27}K into the yardage of a solar system's wick
Of matter! Why banter further about how it is said?
It is as important as my equestrian trash (Alpha Centauri)
As I carefully clothe myself upstream in a silken sari
From Andromeda. At three minutes and 10^{9}K, in a bed
Of protons and neutrons fusing to atoms, I quickly shed
My will to be quite objective, even in my candidly sorry
State of flux at 10^{5} years and 3000K in a faint slurry
That I admire for the fusion PKS2000–330 that once led
To quasars somewhere at the rim of this human universe.
Such correspondences do not make a good thing worse,
But show only that the mind must sparkle and rehearse
The consistent gift of one's translation as a verse
That Elohim inspirited: $I = i \times i^{3}$, that is I AM,
Though not as sadly as one who says, "Sing it again, Sam"
And mists into darkness a little perplexed. My Word!
All this at the edge, so white and downy and moving
Away in the past of billions and billions of light-years
At ninety percent of the speed of light, our fears

Askance, beyond our knowing and beyond our proving.
The grid of space is internal, in the yearning that tears
Must inspire, to see, to know in the light of the weirs
Of gravity. And we, in this near situation, improving
Our lot like one Candide, are all we see. What lies
In the mind as a force that receives the Unified Field
In its cooling expansion? Surly logic that tries
The depths of time encases experiments that yield
Only shadows of ourselves. What is out there
That is not in here? It is only that we somehow care
To see the stars and quasars in their sheets of blue,
Tint of starlight scattering dust, and there! slow
Tau Ceti, Lalande, Cygni, Luyten, Ton, the hue
Of Virgo, Indus of the supercluster, Coma, and Virgo
Low in the air and dwelling in, on the tip of the tongue
As the Word.

TO THE PHARAOH–HUNTER K ORION

[See commentary]

Supernal hieroglyph of the hunter-warrior,
O Ramses, evocative constellation in your sway
Over these stars, you come as a venerable courier

Of Ra at night to stand forth as if at day
Against the underworld. You move as on a spindle,
Passing overhead, autumn to autumn, in the play

Of the oversoul. That dark Anubis must dwindle
And not stay. But your Bellatrix, Betelgeuse,
And Rigel stay starry full over the brindle

Sand of starpoint pyramids in the ruse
Of immortality, brandishing forward blue-white
Gemstones in that setting. What is there to lose

But glory, to think of the wash of satin in the flight
Of river-wings of falcons rising softly into mist
And corona of the moon? O Egypt, in the sleight

Of living that favors immortality, the far bell
Of windsong arrives among the columns of Abu Simbel
To touch the fleeting spirit with its fleeting knell.

There is no pain. Wrought gold lies over the fell
Visage that is decay. The voice of artifice will tell
Of your dynasty with eloquence as in a dell

Where the golden visage is sure, whose eyes clear
Where the empire of darkness yields the weir
And net of stars to the Fisherking. He sheds a tear

For you, who strode before him as the mighty seer
Of Ra, who saw his coming in the hieroglyphic mere
That is the heavens, there and there in the sheer

Darkness over us. It will shimmer and appear
Above the sands of Egypt, eternally without loss,
In another vision, within the Southern Cross.

RAMSES II OF EGYPT

Before me is the length of the Nile and two lands
Inviting the reign of Amun Ra in his pharaoh
Of the sun and the lapis lazuli of the sands

Of Egypt. So I take up the sceptre to harrow
The lands as one, my insight and uraeus
Forward, quick as the quickest eyelet, narrow

To see the will of Amun from golden Sirius,
Star of the endless dynasty. The sparrow
Is not the falcon, and the falcon, curious

In flight, will find the widest domain. Char
And ruins of the past lie against a hill,
And in that repose allow the brightest star

New access to god Amun's brightest will
In the temple's languor of eternal peace
Near the Nile. The star will rise and spill

The brilliance of the golden mien to release
The gold of our desire across the hieroglyph
And flow through it until a hand will crease

Death's linen into darkness even as the sylph
Of light reaches its cloudy height. What is nearer
Than darkest water? There, among the stars, a skiff

Of light will rise and touch the brightening mirror
Overbending us. Great Egypt is the golden land
From which the vision falls away, still clearer

Here as the golden dream and the fire of sand,
The three to five proportion of all experience.
This is the meaning and the image that will stand

The wear of time as it dusts against the prurience
Of death. Know the azimuth, the azure span
Of light, the aureole, and the prescience

Of Amun Ra. I take my sceptre and lift
Its lustre over Africa. I announce the mean
At Abu Simbel in my very image and sift

The winds to come. I keep the lands in the sway
Of record. I am of these people, the mien
Of their desire, the fire of sand, the array

Of light from Amun Ra. I touch the rift
Of sound. I hear god Amun come. I will not stray.
I whisper what I know in silence. The drift

Of time sustains me in my tomb. Death stings
In dark Amenti, but within the falcon's wings
     I am Osiris of the lapis lazuli.

THE CARTOUCHE OF RAMSES II

The senses are the holy seven, as I proclaim:
Sight and sound and hearing and touch and taste
And exopraxis, and infolding time in which I waste
The loss of heavenly Amun, caressing my name
Into stone. The river bends and flows the same,
Whether future or past, into the godly green
Of Osiris, who receives us in the haste
Of our dynasty. Now is the green curve's frame
Of the parallax which I shall bend to follow
The depths of diamonding. Space is the hollow
Of the mind as it floats in the diaphane of tile,
In the myriad and range of color in the Nile
Of hieroglyphs. Time is the line of tallow
Aflame in holy linen that wafts in the timbrel
Gold lifting in folds of stone into the windswell
Over the flooding Nile beyond Abu Simbel and the wings
Of the Falcon as it rises in the valley of the celebrant kings.

MAY: THE ARCHITECT OF RAMSES II

The eye is the aperture of the very sun;
    So concentric rings of circlet stone
    Will bring the sun into the cave of bone
    As the mummy sees, in the dark unknown,
The obelisk rise where great god Amun

Rides the golden blue of the upper rooms
    Of sky. The veiling light hangs here
    From his azimuth, transcribing the mere
    Of sunset red and gold. Later, I peer
Above to see the stars from tombs

In the Valley of the Kings in darkling day!
    Sun so warm and full will surely dim
    The light of the architect but limn
    The angels that here will fall and skim
The mind with variant lines that stay

The compassing. Still, I draw the edge
    And threshold of a tomb to meet
    The light that touches Ramses to delete
    All death. The dead for whom we entreat
Osiris arise the hieroglyphs as from a ledge

I make a place for them for Amun Ra,
    Who will keep them as the king was kept
    From day to day. I bowed and wept
    As Ramses lay unmoving and slept
In prayer to envision what he saw,

Drawing geometric lines that render
    Endless curves, as the Nile bends
    Across the plain of wheat. Starlight wends
    There brighter still, where Ra suspends
Night's sudden vision. See the king as lender

Of Amun's glory! Death is as the caret stone,
    The pyramid, the gleam, the valley's rim
    Across the mounds where the dark will brim
    Into the sky. Amun comes for him
As our geometer where light is sown

And rapt in linen as we pray.

THE HANDMAIDEN OF NEFERTARI

I will go with you and care for you.
   Wings may flutter, but the sound
   Will shimmer in a nearby pond,
Then soften, though our days are few.

O Queen, I know your quiet gaze
   Through shadows where the evening
   Runs like wavelets against seeming
Islands beyond the darkening haze

Of the listing sun. I know that hue
   Against your indigo, swanlight
   Under the azimuth of blue-white
Stars that sink away like rue

That dies in our hands from being taken
   Too quickly in the sun. Long in the sieve
   Of woven gold you remained to live
Till now, and then beyond, unforsaken

Then in Ra. Steady in my gaze
   You shall be still, curved and even
   In a hieroglyph and the seven
Circlets of grace in eternal days

Of beauty for our Pharaoh, whose sway
Is blue-dark night or golden day
Whether we go with him, or stay.

THE PYRAMIDS OF EGYPT

Each from its apex suspends the light of Ra
Down into sand that spreads it, each to draw
The gaze aloft into the clerestories of cloud
Brazen with dusk, as if their planes might flaw

The truth with their variety. Each follows
The light from silver to amber to blue in shallows
Of sky overhead as we, envisioning the eternities
Of their geometry, follow the edging hallows

Of sequestering each pharaoh who lives and lives
To rise from a mummy's steady, gazing eyes
Deep in a tomb. The dynasties were hives
Of the Geometer who offers the spiritus and skives

The light into foil that curls into a gathering skiff
Of cloud to shade the linen across a throne like a massif
For a falcon gliding to an ever higher aerie.
There, in the thinning air, are prisms stiff

With the tectonic discipline that rests as trinity,
The fathering lord, the lordly father of eternity,
And the ghost that slips between as one moves
Before and near and then around in the intensity

Of every light, even in the oceanic blue
That wavers with white to anneal the quiver
Of silver into deeper blue. And then, anew,
The pyramids dream their souls aloft to sue

God Amun for his synchrony with Christendom.

BOUGAINVILLEA: A HISTORIOGRAPHY

If one can sense that space and time can bend
And so return upon themselves to end
Where they began in the round of one consistory,
Then one may know enough to write a history.

In this place of events, the bougainvillea may rise
Like a thread, vining tree or stone, or the fascia
Of mind. Whether one sees it is hardly a notice
To be published in some scholarly gazette in which
The history of the scholarly and steady addresses
The nature of reality, for historians are astute
In withholding waves of calculus as they ascend
The shore of coral reef undersea and slow into white
Tumult, heaving and thinning. Far ashore, the fox
Winks at the evidence; the coyote, low in grass,
Slips forward, bristling, twitching; the bear rumbles
And rolls, mimicking; the deer shudders like aspen;
The wolf skulks like an abbreviation; the thunderbird
Castigates versions of cloud. Time flows in, windless,
Hardly impressing the weathervane of the ghost
Who verifies the real. How may one proceed? Diction
Is the means by which one orders the tools of mind
Or becomes the isle beyond which the sea strives
Over the reef and slips ashore. (What words are these
That reach into experience, admissible in experience
Among those who envassal themselves in perspectives
Of the totem bestiary, narrowing virtues of survival?
See the array chosen from the Latin word hoard
To seize attention of the scholarly! Should one
Continue with them, or shift the sounds to Saxon
And thus admit the versing yeoman of the practical?
Who can omit either?) For all behold the relative waves
Of our shore. One must try the sea, the limitless
Forms, and tiers of blue, envisioning and wresting

Its secrecy into being as a calculus. Why not, then,
The theme of trinity in the triolet. Amen, amen, amen.

It is not a vise, but a way to improve versions
Of the counters that touch rings of the paradigm
That God set forth from his hand. Excursions

Of imagination may tempt the voyager to skim
Immediacy, following a sign to the designs
Of paradise. (One has seen those who must trim

The cloth of logic that sags like descending vines
Heavy with themselves in the province of Rule.
If there is more than the absolute of lines

That do not veer, one should know a way to the pool
Of sleep, or the cognitive. The speed of light
Is the constant in the stir of the final school

Through which one moves, preparing himself to indict
The world, his medium.) Bougainvillea touches stone
But holds, lissome under derisions of the kite

That, as if an eagle, carks in the eerie zone
Of elision. History is the complete disclosure,
Not the rime of intellect that erects the cone

Of uncertainty. Bougainvillea wavers like the lure,
Or the allure, of the imago made from translucent deity.
Its faery being, blossoming, casts itself as if to stir

The air with frost of light. If one achieves velleity,
He may spin into an image that conveys itself beyond
Limited space into the endless time of propinquity.

God made poetry as the imago of imagination to astound
The physicist, to make him contrite within the compass
Of his own delusions. Historians are so, profound

With slight impediments, dulling opaque in the impasse
Of their theory. Imagination is a pool that transliterates
Heaven more real than ever: see the highborne pass

Above the clouds, far away, as if it waits
To spend its radiance into the authentic curve
Of time as an intimation. One must abandon traits

Of disunity; God dispenses quantum time to serve
Propinquity. One cannot sense God's end of time;
One cannot sense that space, though it may swerve

Through gravity, is endless. Near the far chime
Of light, in its synesthesia, all can be one,
As the theistic light avers in cogent rime,

The tercet that lends eternity. But sensing it
Lies beyond the mind, in faith. Bald historian
Cannot fathom it, though he may prance with wit

And generate another tome like a Victorian
Who, considering alternatives, must knit
His logic to his sentiment. Such a Pretorian

Must guard his protohistory, what he erects
As objectivity, though arcane knowledge wends
Along a stem to flow into greening synthesis,
Though he seems to wink, bristle, twitch, rumble,
Roll, shudder, and skulk with all he knows,
Under heart-shaped leaves.

I AM OM
[See commentary]

Some say that om is very much like ohm,
But a Hindu ecstasy has merit such as in
The Taj Mahal, all white, or like crepine,
Overlaid in air. I am is at home
With it, as in I am that I am, or even loam
Lacustrine with lilies enough to win
A faith. I would not even put a jinn
So far away as not to be amenable. I roam
Like a gazelle astride in and over belief,
Trying so for the time of trying to stay
The modicums of tendency that I should pray
A moral tune. That great author of relief
Will begin a trend to apprehend a glory
That rests inside and all around like a story
Of a maker who would tell us why, and how,
We should believe to favor Him.

IMAGES OF GOD

To the Newtonian of consequence, the Word follows
The sinuous vine. It grows in nook and cranny,
As Tennyson saith. Where is the tendril, uncanny
With its bloom? It touches the very mallows
Of light, ochre in brown and turquoise as hallows
Of gold supervene. The gorgeous dawn, homey
With green, yields la vie en rose, with tallows
Of gold in its reprise. Who might instruct Adonoi
In this, with reason? Reason is what one makes of it,
With spirit, if you will, or variegations of wit,
Not with emplaning Germanic prose, but for the roi
Who is sun, affecting the sun. Even sovereign
Louis of France had it right, right as serein
Of the sun at dawn to bless and be blessed, contrite,
Not contrarily, but like great Ramses of the chariot.

THE FIRST PRINCE

The flow of sound is the flow of color.
There! The bright burst of red,
The violet wind, the silent shred
Far too far to hear. In the dolor
Of murmuring covenants of the solar
Earth, you, in your resurrection, shed
Restriction as you try the mead
Of darkness between the polar
Stars. Hear the distant soul
Resplendent in the falls of light
Beyond the apertures of sight!
You are He afar, beyond the shoal
Of our being, among meadow flowers
That are strewn across the showers
Of light that fall to us.

An Intimation of the Lord Jesus Christ . . .

HELLO

Walking intently through passages of sun,
He keeps a rare pale light around his face
As if he had decided how very well at eighty
He should be, or how immortal. I saw him
Pass into the north as if it were a transept
Of morning, where homes abide in fields
On either side of the street. He was alone,
Separated from care around the corner, east.
So I found it in myself to keep concern afresh,
Though the silence was pure as the sound in trees,
As leaves kept court, and birds were heralds of weather.
I went to the wooden bridge and looked after him
As if expecting him to rise through fallow light
Into the heights of meadowland and cirrus petals
Of cacti pale from dew. But he had turned back,
And I met him, at a distance, with an easy "hello."
He came immediately to me, with the somnolence
Of whitest white, his hair luminous as frost
In the aureate white of his belief, knowing me,
And concerns of immediate history in the fief
Of his sentences. The counters of his meaning
Feathered his intonations until what he quickly said
Was dressed for the panoply of the clouds and hill
And the vast estate of spring behind him, dazzling
The skiey daffodils across the fence and grasses
Of its verdure. He wondered how all were, here,
In the field of willows. And I saw, in his report
Of disciples, what he must leave them, even now,
Before his transpiring more fully as a persona
Of his own events. What can remain but events
That pile over each other, stone upon stone, rising
As a wall? His spirit fled in the blue-white
Wind, and wings invested the leaves, busy

With experience. The lean philosopher would know
The pillow of his presence, historian the bleak
Accoutrements of awareness and the fobs of thought
That pile forth into the conscience, constricting
The nets of what he meant: the presence increate
In the space around us, murmuring with silence—
He and I, together, he in his witness, I in mine,
Understanding the pause in silence, the diamant
Clasp, and the weave of the prism's spectrum
Passing into the presence of words.

THE UNSEEN WORLD

It lies behind you, motionless as fear,
Like larvae sinking into sleep, rapt,
And dreaming rigidly of flight and flame;
It lies apart, aside, unseen, for what
Remains is husk, the stiffening cocoon;
It lies behind you, hidden in the sheath
Of anonymity, crisp, the laughing sum
That slips like light in air, around and in,
Flown and borne, of being winging full;
It lies behind you, motionless as fear,
Arranging in the forms its core of mind
That binds the seen unbreathing as a tomb.

THE MORNING OF THE FIRST RESURRECTION

The suns of topaz pearl tourmaline strontium
Agate crystal quartz, of light cerise gemming
Sunrise grain indigo and carmine stars
East north east lining in, dispersing
To circumference and horizons round
And stars at the elevation of sunrise
At degrees near twenty-five for the shadowless
Day and the circumference of vision and angels
Helming the spectra in. Morning is awash,
Flowing in the icy caverns of supernal dark,
The lancets of sapphire therefrom calling
Suns that vanquish the meridian as Polaris
Rings the vision. The final light has come
As day. When in the tales of the millennium
Was this told candidly? Though words
Express the edifice now that Isaiah and John
Of Revelation mount the clouds as if they were hills,
The fantasies of realities confirm theme
And veriest hint in the surge of the dawn of glory.
Messier 81 stands away, and Andromeda wears
The Spiral Galaxy. Constellations of the Cross
Invade the spatial dark, and light is the ring
Of gravity that drew us, always curious, in.
This majesty is the kindness of beatitude
And the versions of the grain. Vibrations
Still awareness, fall away, tremble imperception,
And ultraviolet is newest color, timbre in sound
Of an echoing flute, far away. Mists of belief
Flow into testament. Then the circumferences
Of the suns become corona, crown, and the Lord,
As intimate as prayer, becomes the image
Of the cruciform of stars. And He will speak
The power of the resurrection when all may follow Him.
All hallows always were of Him, now fully seen,
Wending from Gethsemane and the prayer of sacrifice
Into the time of space and space of time unending.

PSALM OF THE LAST JUDGMENT

You know the near, the very near as you scan
The shadowed hemispheres nearby. Your vision
Closes near upon you as you whisper and repine
In folds of my sequestering. Now, in the quelling
Sleek of utter night, I give you the curve Orion
And little more. The light of far galaxies
Is lost, having fallen quite away, forever
Gone. I heard it going like a mere whisper
Purling in an eddy of this great galactic sea.
All else was lost thirty billion years ago,
And what you see of stars is the fragile memory
I have given you for circlet seeing. I see like you.
You feel the knowledge that stars have vanished
In the sky of death you know above a silent
Sea. What you are is of my fold and my awakening.
I am all you have, your brother. Take my hand
In the utter void. I hover here in the radiation
Of all the light there is. I am the light of the world,
And the world is but a grain, though imperative to me.
I have remained to help you slowly to your knees.
I have knelt in prayer in this vast abyss,
Unbreathing, but sustaining you. Bring your charm
And trinkets with you, and some heavier elements
That you have gathered from these nearby nebulae.
Come to Alpha Centauri, now, and I shall explain
Further how we are one, alone and whispering
Our decision to live beyond the sun's remaining fire.

APOCALYPSE

Song
            smooths
                        vitreous song
Emerging from the potter's clay
Waterleafing
            star
                        arc of supernal awe
Variegated
            in the solemnity
                        of the lofty vision
Measureless containment
            over the star
                        the starry fields
And furling clouds
            laminae of time
Song of an echo
            echo over echo fleeting
                        solace of the wheeling
Variances
            penumbras
                        meadows of darkness
Measureless
            and empty
                        but dust
Tinkles in a vision
            of knowing
                        lost in the concert
Of stars
            liquor of light
                        cursive and burning
In the urgency
            of song
                        song of ellipses

Cleft
        in the air
                of one song
Diurnal spring
        of the arousing day
                after the yield
Of afternoon
        as the impresario
                of laughter
Laughter
        light
                in the sea
Vitreous fire and light
        agar
                light

THE BLACKSMITH'S FORGE

Coke coals gleamed from the bellows air,
Sparkling tiny comets to the blackdust
Walls and floor, steady to the anvil that rang
Rough song.

The blacksmith, aproned in leather,
Bent over the fetlock, hoof in hand,
Sledging nails and biting them in proper.

The grime, except in the stress of flame,
As if it were the mere leaven or savoring,
Flowed like a hymn among the morphous iron,
And this, arranged and scrutable, was meant for all,
To be worn as plows and rakes among the hay,
All for harvest autumn.

The forge smoke,
Warm and slightly nimbus everywhere,
Drew our ardor new among the trees
And alleys of our young careers; so
Rapt, we watched his purpose work in steel,
Bright in a shoe,
The flow of his thorough yield.

Who else could forge the spray
Of novae for our feet where all was splendor,
Silken and rococo, from his firm and ample hand?

THE SONG OF LIGHT

I

Listen! Over the arch of silence that shrouds the mind . . .
Listen! In the quiet hour, when we sit and wait,
When the leaves flicker in the dark wood where we walk,
And the light is hushed, and the trees grow dim,
The spirit whispers like the conscience of Him.
Listen! In the vale of hours we hear the murmur of wings,
In the sky the silvering stars, and we wonder, in love,
    that love can be
We leave the street, the road, the path,
And push the leaves aside, and there in the gold and green,
The green and gold, are the sunlight and shade,
And the spirit listens, and the spirit speaks.
Listen! The brightness is the sunlight gold,
The hovering warmth, the quietness.
In the glades the swallow whispers.
Wait for the voice that comes;
Wait for the voice of the leaves.

II

The air is the motion of mind.
Over the air is the voice of light,
Where the stars open the canopy of night.
Over the air, over the wood, the sunburst God must reign.
The quietness, the quietness, where we push the dim lore
Of our days aside or where we hold them, and look,
And ask them to be what they were.
We have taken them and have made them streets
Of exchange, or a fair for the storm of our interchange,
Until in the storm we fail and wander.
Over the air is the voice of light
Where the stars open the canopy of night.

:

III

We have marshalled history where we reign.
We have called the thoroughfare our home,
The buildings of trade our palaces,
And what we wish to hear we hear,
Average and plain, average and near.
We have wandered in cities, away from home.
See, the spire, the chapel of trees, the lake!
Listen! The hours break, and we look up from the pages
    of our ritual
To see the lake and the shore!
The willows rustle with wings.
Hear! The green and gold, the shade is near,
And where we stand we speak!
"Spirit of leaves, of water and air,
We are here, where the streets end
And we stand silent with love!"
The azure and the flickering green,
The sheen of days, and we come!

IV

The down of cottonwoods, the rivers of trees,
The basking fields, and the meadows of gold . . .
Listen! Summer is the glow, the air is warm,
And the swallow wheels and lilts through light.
The points of wings, and it is gone!
We have felt the smooth flight, the flight of God,
And the play in the dusk of afternoon,
Hidden where we hold ourselves alone.
This part of us we do not devote to scales and measures
                that yield us open everywhere
And so make us the distances of what they are.
We have held ourselves in pain away,
Frightened under the glaze of discipline
And the gaze of what we thought we were.

V

We have met Jehovah on a page, in a verse or line.
We have met Him in the past, in prophets and the weirs of truth.
These we have taken and espouse,
These we bear as vessels of antiquity,
And these we speak. These are sure.
But at the edge of the lake the air shimmers
As with the quickness of a hand or wing!
We have met Jehovah on the page of prayer,
Over the desire that He may be.
We have sought Him plainly in what we know,
But have not known ourselves,
The flickering light that tells us yes or no.
Meet Him there, the image of the singing air!

VI

Conscience, voice, or being of the lake,
The softness tells us He is here!
Look in upon the vast realms of all man is,
Look in and wonder where the hours fell,
And why, so perilous and gray, still they fall away,
Gray and taken by the day.
Listen! The azure voice is near,
Speaking, speaking in our fear
That we can hear!

VII

It is the belling tine within,
The voice that keeps us what we are,
Steady as the day, steadier than all we know.
Jehovah, speak within!
The steady, silver mien,
The whisper, "Come!"
And here the cruciform that He might be,

The tree of light that stands within,
The life and light of men.
Listen! Over the arch of silence
There is no silence, but the voice;
There is no voice but light,
The rivers in trees, the shimmering gold,
The lake, and the azure years!

ADVENT
[See commentary]

The gentle God is our guest:
His staff will prompt us to the door.

The table is set in the oak-paneled room:
Goblets are rinsed and set out,
The warm vapor vanishing around them:
The silver, withdrawn from felt-lined red mahogany,
Is counted and burnished to mercurial white
And set on immaculate linen,
Sleek with crystal and rococo ware.

The table is set for the Guest
Near the imminent door.
The servants stalk
Each gray indiscretion to be rent
On the merciless rack of their decor.

The table is set for the gentle God:
The roasted fowl entice the savoring tongue:
The marmalade and sweetmeats brim
The centerpiece, a horn;
The fruit is full, plucked in prime,
Oranges, apples, pears
Like noon-shade autumn leaves.
The supper will please the gentle God
Who surely comes,
Who comes like the breath on a veil.

But out of the East the breath is fire!
Who comes with temblor, sound of hurricane?
Who rages on the portico?
Who claps his vengeful steel on stone?
Who comes to dine?

The servants cower like quail in the anterooms.
Who blasphemes in the shuddering halls?
Who rends the imminent door?
Our guest is a gentle God, a Lamb.

THE CONVERSIONS OF GOD

West-End Clinic,
or God the Scientist

I

The building with the chrome ceiling, amid the shanties
        of the natural world,
Where the people come
To get their absolution, rid of God:

Consider the toad's eye in the wet morning,
        beside the pool from which it came.
The empirical day arrives in the brainpan:
Zit, and the neurons spark responsively,
For this we know above all else,

Or rather this is all that can be known,
The Soul, Phenomena.

Stretch out here:
We find the ceiling reflective in this clear light,
        helpful for syntheses.
Take this vine of nerves and the prose response,
Zit, and we know! Wondrous!
The conscionable method, the Christianly practicability.
Say to me, vine, what concerns you,
That I may sense the orange pain
Where saffron eddies like the nebulae under my thumb.

This is my scalpel, the extensive finger of my sense
Where pain dies from pain,
Where excision is the definition and name;
As I am
I am,
Contained in the divisible light before the prism of my eye.

Say to me, vine, what invades you,
And I shall subtract it from you
And a little of you from you,
And so cleansed and made more pure,
You shall become more the light, the simple light
By which I see, less various, more like the essence of me,
The simple truth, the measure of white fact,
God, the Frost.

II

In the temple of even stone, the ceiling glitters down,
And I see the image of me at large in heaven,
Zit! it is I, glory, the synopticon, the oracle!
Say to me, vine, what mind may know,
And I shall delay the day of the scythe.
Say what you know before the fact that fact may be,
That all superficies may live,
Your hair (tumbling and black as the flowing night),
Your nose (the fleshful orifice),
Your eyes (milk and blue),
And your very skin (the sac of life),
Zit, and you shall live huzzahing, huzzahing
Zit in porcelain:

Nodding to node, anode, cathode, where life flows,
I suture this to that and that to this
And hope they grow, carefully now,
To offer proof, proof
On this altar of the ultimate law.
God! Zit! the light doth flow;
Zit! Ah! find it good!

III

Fancy fancy
Suddenly, right under the mirror we used to scrutinize them,
      the Lady stopped and asked a boy scout of my scientism

if he needed help. Well, he turned around and said,
"Lady, I'm supposed to be helping *you*. Don't encumber
me with your solicitude."
Conceive of this temerity:
The Lady, whom we shall call the intermediatrix for sake of
protocol, waved like a palm and vanished into the sun-
stream of death:
Yahweh, Yahweh, of the mountain and sky comes;
He flames into the hill like a dart awry: ah,
Zit, and the cathodes hum.

    IV

I hear the ashes sift in your composure for afternoon
And eddy through your caverns of cerulean bone:
You are as the veined leaves hustling and shattering
In the red and gold gusts about the vineyard.

My arch delicacy taps your elixir of nerves
And finds you full of prayer as Pentecost with me.
Now dryly shaking, they clack like brittle threads
Appalling the gossamer mind with alien death.

    And she said, holy, holy, holy—
    Hysterectimus, eclectimus.

Now calm the systolic mercury;
Calm the veins of helpless being:
Ease them here, as strands of pain
Fray in the afterlight of my shaded room.
Whisper in the vale of your being,
And easy near the austere counter thrive beyond here,
Where the biochemist greets you, serves you,
Leaning for the invoiced Elohim.

    And the chyme will sing,
    Abba, abba, the pill hath virtue.

Elevatio hostiae:
Take this now, in daily ritual,
Replenished when you come and come again.
Withdraw into the sepulchre of gold,
Shining in your prosthetic sheath of skin.

Kyrie eleison, O Equanil,
Gloria in excelsis deo, deo;
O nil and equal Equanil
Resurgens
In gusts of gold.

I am the vine, ye are the branch:
She that abideth with me, and I with her,
The same bringeth forth much fruit;

Peace I leave with you,
My peace I give unto you,
Not as heaven giveth,
Give I unto you.

    And she said, abba, father,
    All things are possible unto thee.

    V

The glazing of foundries
Distorts the washed interiors
Of shops I gaze into:
I, walker of the pavement,
Cursorily judge and
Decree them a complex of tile
And talk, whited and small.
Inside, where debris,
Tornadic, swirls,
The revolving fans
Sweep above the clientele

Or lifters bulging humble trade.
Outside, I stare at the heat
And startle up the wrappers
Near my feet,
Shuffling like a broom
Where the shops end, for now
The statuary columns
Are cast in gold, the legal good
Transpiring in ledgers
And vaults of the Board.
I stand outside
As the inquirer
Who sees the implacable
Coming of snow,
The day's hauteur
Groaning under the intimation
Of ice and grime.

Beyond the notary's sign,
The dialed vaults,
The desks and stone,
Beyond the shades
And green cabinets,
The cases, aisles,
And partitioned talk,
Cool and ventilated,
Crisp or fine, like
Vellum ledgers caressing palms
And inexorable thumbs,
The exchange grows serpentine.

The city's noon
Fires the roofs
Of outer hell;
The unequivocal
White and violet
Glare over the ovening

Summer buildings
And erode the pale dry rot.
Where the executive
Foxes subtly bark,
The Hunter comes,
The hooves of stallions
Chiming the streets.
Go home, go home
And wait for him;
His blood is on your door.

The Gull,
or God the Philosopher

I

My gull's claws creak, widening like sabred jaws
Against the great ship's deck to show their air-borne mastery,
As if to grasp, arrest, and lift it up,
Sea-turned and swept, for facile scrutiny:
They only mar, dull the gloss it gets by time, mind, and holystone
And nick the natural grain.

II

Like a baleful traveller
I pace the empty station;
I gaze at the bracketing hours
That package departed trains,
And from my red claws
I drag the luggage of my sterling viscera.

Angkor Thom,
or God the Brahmin

I

In an eddy of wilderness and time, the tracery
Of peril rose, the faced stone, the grimace of heaven,
The gates of sandalwood, the heft of prayer:

The long lion and the hyperbolic Rhesus
Guard time and the sluice of meaning;
The dispassionate figurine spares the ineffable hint,
The breath of scent in the lost gardens of earth and time
From which the tiers of gods yet reign, sullen
In quiet war, stone of their fury, relics of medieval lore
From which the makers fled: beasts to the rain forest,
To the arch cobras and the treading lions.

II

Karma
Dissolving, the capsule thought engenders god from the spot
Of mind, the fixation of gathered calm, of shallow breath,
Of the held viscera and the apparent spine.
The spirit lofts from the flesh,
Lost in the analogues or braziers
And the stemmed and petalled truths.

III

One thinks of the unempirical resignation or silence
In the pall of Angkor Thom, the achievement and dissolution:
It came like a hollow mound, facing the clouds and air
Of oblivion and the courts of death.

The stone heads glower, dismembering green waves
Of rain where they are,

But the continent gods hover, wraiths of scent
In the dusk of sandalwood.

The Chain,
or God the Catholic

I

Abbot Aristotle, if you had known! Simple as Paphnutius,
Thom (of Aquino) came, of the geometric argument:
For speculation (not to be taken seriously) may lead
To the wary catechism that may hump like a dragon!

The pain of silence withdrawn in folds of wool,
The lamb of grace appoints the niche of blue prayer
In the half light of the Gothic god
Geometered from nothing, but if philosophy is

Or is in the least real, it must be perfect,
The negation, what God is not,
The reverse and elementary postulate of mystery, darkness.

A moment before, the white dragon
Trekked through Lethe for the Virgin,
Who mounted him in the meadows of sacraments: epiphany.

Now Saint Thom posits the endless chain
And the Index near the ground of God.
Bidden and forbidden, he glows,
A will o' the wisp, but warm with myrrh,
Rapt and cardinal.

Can one be taken seriously?
The Virgin hums intimacies beyond one's breath,
In silence. Thom dotters grave and solicitous
Through his dialectic: the pink images smile

In the caves of their being, nodding catechisms
To the tracery of air: yes, if you come, come
Envassaled and easy, eke lovely to me.

II

The maelstrom breathes the night wind:
In the vortex and vales of the sea
The death's head glimmers,
Careening, suspended, wildly searching.
Spirit in me that is all I should have been
And yet is the aspect of me as redeemer,
Rise magnificent in the martial gold,
Rise against the chaos of the sea.
My shoulders move like grain on a hill,
Full and tan mellow;
My arms carry the sheaves;
My hand rests as on a staff;
My hair is the fusion of paths of flame;
And my eyes flicker and play,
And stay the death's head from the imperium of man.

III

I see the death's head swing over the heads of men
Who become the courts of law and the assembly of the
        righteous
To make themselves aware of their virtue and fondle it;

They find their rigor and anoint it well,
The unction thick and satisfying,
Greasy from the decadence of flesh.
What they feel of the blue hyacinth,
They erect in iron in the vestibules
Where they dourly advise the young.
The lowered voice impedes the breath;

The scent of goldenrod is gone:
Into the high valley the grey wind comes
Like the creeds of believers.

But in whom can one believe?
The misers of their estimate of good
Bequeath the laurel to themselves,
Bawling righteousness among the cliffs,
That echo again, again.

Gothic Ulm,
or God the Protestant

     I

Let us take a text: the kindness of God is a feather
That graces the square churches
Where we adjust our consciences and speak
Of the tremulous spirit of truth:

I am the lap of the renaissance,
The suspicion of God.

     II

The children of our pedantry sit
Corporeal and negroid in the typical gown,
Tasselled and mortared to listen—
To listen always
Like a mute and collective Gorgon
Brought endlessly under the devotional Novocain.

The sermon grows from the podium
Like old adhesions in the body clergic;
Used and used again, the phrases
Arise, centuries old, from the sea of plasmic survival.

The speculative core of man evolves
Like his durable loins,
And the inestimable animal world repines
And dies
In fear of the god that made boredom immortal.

III

But gather in this ravine where the dry hills bleach the sky.
When morning came, we were young as when it spills rain;
Now, in the firelight, the ghost above me glows and flickers
In a frame of sky above the emerald coasts of the inland sea.
The emerald rain, flying against the panes, roottrees,
And doors of wonder, wells, the wind driving it here.
When the rain comes, it sings through me,
Lifting me to Solomon, but now the squall stops at the pass,
The saline dust sifts skyward, glossing the nightsea
Crystals floating there like faith far gone.
I, honest among Calvinists, barely remember my identity
As the sign of rain; how love, when the values come,
Is odd but meaningful.
Now odd and meaningless, it vaguely shifts and cannot be;
I browse forever turgidly, a committed egotist
Shrifting sackcloth as I crowd to lever up communal
Phrases against the hint of laughter or complaint.
Secure, I die unbreathing in my rippling lint.

But fires drive from the sudden ghost who waits
Like a hanging sheet and hunches up, preying;
He tires of the void eyes of Buddha
And his vassals in the fastness of the East.

Now castles build over cumuli,
Archetypes of change gathering where the dry hills
Sun the sky and strange cacti return a trace of rain
To the brilliant air that spills in me, so splendid, newly sane.

The Chieftain,
or God the Father

Epigraph sub rosa:

Gravitation is the positive force of particles exerted more
powerfully at right angles to a magnetic field, which is produced
by the elongation of the electronic mass of an atom; as the electrons
are forced away from the more stable nucleus, they become freer,
and so create fields of attraction and repulsion beyond the nucleus.
Some elements are less amenable to this heretic elongation because
the charge of the electronic shells is minimized because nearer the
principal mass. Magnetism is the false light, specious and temporal:
negation, heresy, and hate; gravity the light and
firmament of love.

I

My ambivalent air rises above the sepulchre
And vanishes like an organ's echo voice
Into the fastness of philosophy.
The chapel is the fastness of a choice
To hear the humming trees and streams, the whir
Of insects wheeling in their noon of ecstasy,
The mountains dark and winding deeper than a prayer.
The guess of truth reigns in the high rock,
Darting where it must remain,
Agile as the denizens of air.
Why must the harder truths the best ones lock,
The truths of subtle ease, of God or bane?

That wisdom sings withdrawn, within the shade.
The song is free, wandering like the cornsilk
Beyond your grasp, thin and fine.
Be quiet, hear. Out there, the honied milk
Of Canaan is in the sky; the humming jade
Of Solomon flushes with his wine.

Nearing, the rapture rests against your ear,
Then seeks you farther in and masters you.
Be still, and wait for evening and its dusky balm.
Be still, for the hours keep you in, against the sheer
Rock you climb. High, you never have known
The man you never were. Du calme, du calme.

II

"Yahweh, you are bound by me, for I, naive
And in your image, am he whom you made.
You invest the air above me, yet would range abroad
And spoil heaven for my joy. I stand with you
Against the vacuum and fires of space,
And you, my elder hand, gather them in,
The fisherman. You make me of yourself
Grown strong, and I, though fainting,
Am drawn up, shaken by your grace.
You are the resurrection whose craft is power,
Whose reason is love, the recessional wonder.

But the binding of light! The rose of conception
Impends like the blue power of stars in your vision,
Spiralling forever away. Yet you stand here
For me, savior.

Yahweh, I shall go to the door and begin.
Here is the ritual of my devotion;
I walk out to the spring where my horse
Bends and drinks from the sky it sees there.
I shall ride the roads of the earth,
Jostling my mettle till it is known
And I gather it as I do these reins.

This you give me as I mount,
Eli, eli, lama sabachthani,
And I go into the white glade where spring comes
In the fervor of love."

III

The magi of palms
Bring them supple in spring
Like the rush of imperishable wings
Into the glade of the god of their praise.
Staid and serious the god, complete

In love, but what he brings is
Like the linnets that skim
Ahead of quickness, the Paraclete!

IV

Suez: where the ships come from the reaches
Of the seas; I watch the sands of Asia shine
In the prism of morning. I, the salvor, align
The compass to my will, stand for the windlass
And crane and the steel maw over water
To salvage incontinent history. The images like coral
Form in the brown sand and hamper the ships.
But the moral of Cyrus is here like the continental divide
Or the new Sierras. I become myself, salvor,
And the ancient is new, rimming my hand.

Should I recall the realm of Pericles as the sand
Of the seaboard wends before my hurricane?
Beyond, Florida and the white avenues, over the tide of time,
Are American, like the plaza of time blue
As the Michigan lakes, the bayous, or the sheen
Of my western arm. But I reach with a crane
To the world of Suez to begin the day of my reign.

V

The ermine sand becomes the faery dust
Of gods reduced to leprechauns by the vast

Attrition of disbelief. It dusts
With the seaward breeze, gauzing the blue air
With thinning mist.

But the day is clear as a tine,
As continental Columbia
Awakening to the westering sun.

The gods lilt among the dunes,
White as spindrift lifting
Washed, baptized, and pure;
Jupiter invades the nuclei
And Poseidon the sea.

Awake and pray:
The titans dance in the cyclotron;
They lift and sail,
Billowing the motion of mind.

Never in the passage of dreams
Were they real as now:
They hint the incalculable god
Wherever they stream
Whose voice is the whisper and ermine of sand.

VI

The moondark cedars keep the whippoorwill,
And I rest awake to the shadow in me;
The white temple lies there,
Waiting in the compass of heaven,
Ghostly in trees,
As I have seen the frieze
Of sunlight in the dust of fields.

Lonely, I walk encumbered
By the ritual of days I have known

Of habitual love;
The vines follow the wall;
The hidden peace began
In the glare of the average sun.

The temple! Rise white and dark,
Near before me and open,
Portals ashen white gold,
Light golden in halls of chivalric kings.
Where are the thousand years
That have brought me here?
Glory and the fall of centuries
Come like the willows' wind.

COMMENTARIES

TO A DYING GIRL   This poem was written about the death of Dyca Ann Frisby Bradshaw, the wife of Larson's friend and former mission companion, Blair. On one occasion when the poet visited the couple in Salt Lake City, she complained of vague pains; soon after, she died of cancer. The poem was not written until eight years later, in 1955, when, in the poet's words, it "came in a rush."

As Eugene England points out in an unpublished article, Larson had been reading Thomas Mann's novella "The Black Swan" and probably also recalled Mann's "Death in Venice," with "the gondola moving in premonition, and like a swan, across the water. And he probably intuited the connection to the Orpheus and Eurydice myth about the strange border between life and death, which will not yield ultimately." The swan has always been "directly associated with beauty and poetry, but especially death . . . . It is the vehicle of the soul's journey after death and thus of resurrection," and the mirror becomes representative of "wisdom, particularly that which has the brightness of eternal life, and . . . reveals whether the soul has lived virtuously." In using these images, the poet "posits the possibility . . . that in her quick going, so painful and troubling to us, she may as quickly forget both the passage the swans have taken her through and also the terribly cold but still *fragile* (temporary) snow of mortal life as she enters the always repeating, mirrored spring of eternal life and eternal lives."

MAIDEN   When he published this poem as part of his "Romaunt of the Rose: A Tapestry of Poems," Larson titled it "Herrick's Julia." The simpler title "Maiden" serves, of course, to stress its universality.

JESSE   Based on the life and ultimately the death of a cousin, "Jess" Green, who lived in American Fork, Utah, and with whom the poet had frequently enjoyed horseback rides to Utah Lake. Young Jess was accidentally shot and killed while Larson was on his mission to England. The incident was especially tenacious in the poet's mind because he had been disturbed by a premonition of Jess's death, yet did not mention it to his cousin. In Eugene England's words, "Larson's awareness of life's absolute boundary is clearly present in the remembered youth as well as in the poet, . . . yet the reality beyond that boundary is affirmed in the created conviction of hope in Christ." The poet has changed the exact nature of the shooting accident in order to get deeper poignancy and to expand the thematic possibilities.

HOMESTEAD IN IDAHO   This often-anthologized poem was based on an actual occurrence which the poet found reported in some genealogical collections from Idaho. The skillful use of the dramatic form provides aesthetic distance but at the same time adds intensity and poignancy to what might otherwise be a simple anecdote.

AN OLD ATHLETE SPEAKS OF HIS SON   The speaker in the poem is the poet's father, Clinton Larson, who excelled particularly in the high jump. After winning a national collegiate championship in Philadelphia, he went to Europe with the A. E. F. In 1919, The Inter-Allied Games were held at Paris, games where leading athletes from around the world participated. On this occasion, the poet's father won first place in the high jump, a feat which, under the circumstances, was recognized as winning the world championship.

CARDING   This poem, honoring one of the poet's colleagues, is a prime example of the way in which he can take a simple pun and expand it into a poem of depth and finesse. Recognizing that Orea Tanner had a gift for inspiring students who had talent but insufficient motivation, Larson begins with the pun that the students are "woolgathering" but he ends by looking at the process which can turn their gathered wool into a significant product.

CHAIRMAN OF THE ENGLISH DEPARTMENT   This poem focuses on the facts that Richard Cracroft's primary concern is the literature of the American West and that his favorite author is undoubtedly Mark Twain.

ELY CATHEDRAL   This poem is best understood and appreciated, I believe, in the light of an experience Larson had when visiting the cathedral, as he recounted it in a published essay. When strolling around the interior, he was struck by the size and location of the gigantic wooden lantern.

> I noticed an old brass plate imbedded in the floor. On it was an engraved cross about three feet long. Scrutinizing it, I saw some small business was at the base of the cross. It was about two inches high and at first looked like a depiction of rubble. Practically kneeling, I saw that it was really a miniature design of the Ely Cathedral itself! The engraved cross rose from its apex—that is, from the lantern. This depiction, it seemed to me, contained the spiritual purpose not only of the lantern but of the Cathedral as well.
>
> The lantern, as I have said, is 170 feet above the floor of the octagon. Looking up again, I saw that it held the base of the spiritual cross of the depiction I had just seen on the floor, for Ely an upright cross as well as the earth-bound cross of the transept and nave.
>
> Consider this. If the lantern is thirty-five feet in diameter, then it would represent the base of the upright of the spiritual cross, and would be a rendering of the diameter of ten inches of the real cross, a scale of about one to forty-two. If the cross of Jesus was about fourteen feet high, then the height of the spiritual cross of Ely would be the relationship of 10 is to 420 as 168 is to X. The spiritual cross of Ely Cathedral, which of course would be impossible to build, can be construed to be over one mile high! How glorious the lantern of Ely Cathedral was to those who conceived of it and built it and worshipped under it! What a magnificent commitment it represented! Looking up again, I felt the tremendous majesty, glory, and gravity of Ely's spiritual cross. Then, in my mind's eye, I could see Ely Cathedral and its spiritual cross as they might be seen as one approaches them along the highway from Cambridge or London.

A BOX OF CHOCOLATES   The subject and tone of this poem can best be appreciated in light of the fact that the poet himself is not merely an unregenerate chocoholic but one of the most dedicated admirers of chocolate-dippers in Western America.

FRED ASTAIRE AND GINGER ROGERS   The poet's obvious delight in the dancing of this renowned couple is neither feigned nor passing. In fact, so profound an influence did Larson's first acquaintance with their movies have on him that he included in his university course work a class in tap dancing.

ASCENT FROM A DIVIDER   This poem was prompted by the poet's learning how concrete freeway dividers have been carefully engineered to provide maximum prevention of a head-on collision. The gradual curving of the base of such a divider is shaped somewhat like a plowshare; the function of this hollow-ground surface is to lift the front end of a car that wanders too far to the left, raise the car, then turn it back into its own lane, on the obvious assumption that a multicar accident with all vehicles traveling the same direction is preferable to a head-on crash.

SEVEN-TENTHS OF A SECOND   This short poem was occasioned by the poet's reading that in a head-on crash or a one-car collision with a fixed object, all the types of havoc detailed here would take place within the limited time defined in the title.

QUIRKY QUARKS   In this science poem Larson reveals his penchant for having fun with all dimensions of words, including phonemes and punctuation as elements in the act of creation. The quark as the fundamental particle of which larger particles are built appears in the opening line as a period. But as quarks combine, they cause a radiating outward and also ultimately lead to the forming of vast units like stars (the asterisk), the solar system (the lower-case o) and finally the galaxy, the full-rounded universe (the capital O). In the same way, particles of sound and meaning gradually develop to structure the fundamental, universal space/time continuum ("updownwhen inout Oh O $E=mc^2$").

THE TWIN PLANETS   The earth and its moon are here presented as counterbalanced twins, an analogy enhanced by the descriptions and photographs of moonwalkers. A favorite theme since their views of the blue planet from space has been the love with which we must treat our fragile unique source of life. In this poem Larson had already presented the contrast of the dead world with the living and, in a manner frequently found in his poems, contrasts the goodness of the light, warmth, and life of our world with the cold, aridity, and spiritual death of our "twin."

THE DARK PLANET: A PROSPECT OF THE END   An apocalyptic poem suggesting the total helplessness inevitable in our world if the inhabitants were to become aware of an approaching mass comparable in size to that of our own planet. A potential means of destruction occasionally suggested by those interested in how the world will end becomes a source of a new type of light; with his characteristic understatement, Larson allows this concluding image to become associated with the cleansing fire of scripture.

ADONOI OF THE CREATION   A bold experiment in the union of scientific jargon with poetic expression. Larson starts the poem with the modern astrophysicist's description of the Big Bang, but it is ironically Adonoi (Christ) who is speaking long after the fact. The fact that Adonoi uses the terminology of the scientific theory in order to describe the event of creation suggests that the important element is not the language which describes what happened, but the later recognition of why and how it happened. Adonoi seems to be saying that the scientist can show vast ingenuity in recreating the timing of events in the immediately post-creative universe, putting times and sizes into negative powers of 10, and temperatures into vast amounts definable only in positive powers of 10. If these figures are combined with a favorite mythic description of creation (the egg of the world), we are left with a fantastically hot omelet ("this omelet grilling at 10^{-32}, a mere tick"). The exact description itself is not the most important element ("Why banter further about how it is said?"). The truly important thing is to see the Creator within the means of creation, whether we call it the Big Bang or something else. What we ultimately find is the creation of something which is tangible from something which cannot be described or defined; the "real" number *one* (here represented by its roman form *I*) can be made from the "imaginary" numbers *i* and i^3. We are abruptly brought back to the person of the Creator by his pun "My Word."
    The net effect of all this should be for us to recognize a Unified

Field not merely in the physical processes by which the Big Bang could bring the entire universe into existence but to recognize also the need for a deeper unity linking the physical, the personal, and the spiritual: "What is out there / That is not in here?" We want to see the physical evidence ("the stars and quasars in their sheets of blue"), but they dwell ultimately "in, on the tip of the tongue / As the Word." Through this type of approach to his subject, Larson is thus able to correlate the creativity of the scientist and the poet with that of the ultimate Creator.

To the Pharaoh–Hunter K Orion   Larson was struck by the fact that Ramses II is portrayed most frequently standing in a hunting stance that is an exact mirror–image of the Greco-Roman constellation Orion (the "K" of the title is an alphabetic approximation of that shape).

I Am Om   A poem of tolerance. Here Larson shows his tolerance in cultural and religious terms and also his constant search for parallels. First, of course, in a somewhat playful verse he makes use of accidental sound-analogies (I AM for the Old Testament creator; OM, the sacred syllable of Oriental devotion; OHM, the modern scientific jargon). Then he begins looking for what joins human causes rather than what can be used to aggravate differences. The result is one of his many poems unifying the ultimate transcendent idealism of Christian belief with similar transcendent spiritual idealisms wherever they are found. The goal, of course, is not to attempt to transform the Taj Mahal into a Christian chapel nor to alter Christianity into a derivative of Hinduism, but to try to give as deep a meaning as possible to the nearly universal concept of the total brotherhood and sisterhood of humanity.

Advent   Here the poet stresses one side of Christ which is often ignored: his masculine strength as judge and avenger. Like the priest who serves as speaker within the poem, many believers see only the meek, long-suffering aspects of God. Certainly, when Christ does come again many who observe ritual for its own sake and who sentimentalize faith will find themselves as bewildered as the persona of "Advent."